The Rhythm of the Christian Year

Emil Bock

The Rhythm of the Christian Year

Renewing the Religious Cycle of Festivals

Floris Books

Translated by Maria St Goar

Fifth edition published in 1992 under the title
Der Kreis der Jahresfeste by Verlag Urachhaus
First published in English in 2000 by Floris Books
Reprinted 2001

British Library CIP Data available

ISBN 0-86315-308-9

Printed in Great Britain
by Cromwell Press, Trowbridge

Contents

Preface

For many years and with special dedication, Emil Bock again and again explored new ways to convey a deepened under- standing of the Christian festivals. He sought for effective indi- cations that would lead to their renewal that is necessary today. Thus, in the course of many years, he wrote quite a number of articles for the monthly magazine *Die Christengemeinschaft* (The Christian Community). In many instances, they were adapta- tions of talks he had given at an annual festival. Important Christological principles and views were developed and brought to life by him in this context.

It corresponds with an intention by Emil Bock during the last year of his life and the wish of his readers to gather these festi- val-essays together in book form and shape them into a unified effect. From single building blocks, a whole has thus been formed that embraces the full circle of the Christian festivals throughout the year.

The Christian festivals from Christmas, Epiphany through Easter, Ascension, Whitsun all the way to St John's Tide and Michaelmas are woven like a golden thread into the rhythmic sequence of the year's seasons and the life processes of the whole earth-organism. Both are intimately linked together. Attentively living with the year's course can guide us to a deep- ened celebration of the festive periods; inversely, we can acquire a new relationship to nature's growth, blossoming, ripening and wilting through a more conscious experience of the festivals. New impulses for people's social life can grow from a regenerated form of celebrating the festivals. But above all, this practising experience and celebration the annual festivals will lead to comprehension of the Christ Mystery of our time. And that is the new Christmas event, namely, the revelation of Christ in the etheric world, a world filled with the pulse of rhythmic life processes. Rightly experiencing the cycle of the year can be a way of accessing Christ's living work as Lord of the Elements, Lord of Life and the heavenly forces on earth.

This book hopes to serve this goal.

Second Coming of Christ: From Faith to Vision

The tender quiet of Advent and childlike bliss of Christmas are gifts of Grace which are granted our age ever more rarely. Life has become too noisy and hectic, fate too harsh and dramatic. Yet, the secret of Advent's quiet can be compared with the sensibility of a woman about to become a mother. The hope embodied in this sensation does not relate to a neutral event that will ultimately occur. Indeed, the woman who carries a child does not merely look forward to an event that will take place in due time. Early on, she is constantly enveloped and surrounded by the soul of the being whom she is allowed to offer a body. In our age, the same change comes to pass which the pregnant mother has to undergo when the calm months of anticipation are replaced by the labour of childbirth. She gladly suffers all the pains and fearful tribulations because she knows they serve her own hope. Today, destinies overcome us that are nothing less than birth pangs passing through humanity. We must give birth to something new that serves the purpose of our salvation. A new Christmas event is imminent in our age for which we have to prepare.

Christ does not come to mankind if calmness reigns. When he appeared two thousand years ago in earthly-human form, calmness likewise did not reign. Those were times of feverish agitation and harrowing oppression. Then too, humanity suffered the pangs of a new birth. More so today, storms of a new birth rage through the world wherein something struggles to come to light. The saying, 'Where suffering is greatest, God's help is nearest' is truly a Christ-related word, for when suffering is at its worst, it is possible to discern from this that he is drawing near who comes for the salvation of mankind.

It would be well if people would not so quickly forget what moved their souls when bombs fell, houses collapsed and cities went up in flames. A destiny of revelation broke in upon us. Its meaning does not lie in the destruction; it lies in what is rising behind it but is concealed from human sight for the time being. A clarion call by God continually goes out to us. But what happens if the one who is being addressed does not hear? It is like this even among us humans; if we want to tell a person something and he or she does not listen, we have to speak louder. So how can clamorous humanity hear what must be said to them? People can only hear something if one yells at them. Applying this to the overall view of things, this is what we confront in our age.

God's quiet speech, his harplike call, has assumed the character of a trumpet in our time and the walls of Jericho have begun to tumble down. Two thousand years ago, a man who towered above his contemporaries appeared before humanity: 'Change your thinking, for the Kingdoms of Heaven are at hand.' Today this is likewise being said, but not by a human being nor even by enlightened humans. Their speech is replaced by that of higher spirits who guide and shape destiny. Destiny calls out to us in trumpet-sounds: change your thinking; for Christ has drawn near! Herein lies the actual discrepancy between today's world view and reality. Destiny speaks, but who is the destiny? When destiny speaks, a spiritual world speaks; lofty, earnest messengers of God speak who belong to the hierarchies of heaven.

The advantage in our age is that the forces of destiny are in the very midst of us and speak to us with utmost directness. But in our heads live thoughts of a kind as if a supersensory world did not exist. In regions untouched by the upheaval of war, one can afford to be a materialist. In the fate-laden parts of Central Europe, destiny refutes the materialistic world view. Destiny makes manifest the actuality of a supersensory world: that supersensible world breaks in upon us. The catastrophes, conflicts, tensions, wars and the clamour of battles that occur among us are not the totality of all that occurs. It is merely the bottom edge. What gives our era its actual content takes place above our heads. Where we do not look, there, the most important events take place.

Christ reveals himself anew. The sphere that is his kingdom presses near, even as the sea comes roaring in over dry ground when ebb-tide is over and flood-tide sets in. Above our heads the spheres move. But we do not see and recognize the world in which the true happenings of our days take place. We are merely puzzled about shadowy outlines, wonder at the strange darkness that falls. We do not see the light that rises behind the clouds and throws these shadows. How can we break the dark spell that confines our insight, vision and perception to the world of the senses and causes us to sleep through the major event of our time?

When the first Christ-event occurred two thousand years ago, the most exalted being whom we call Christ, in his infinite mercy and benevolence clothed himself in earthly visibility when he incarnated as man. Thus, his contemporaries saw Christ with their earthly eyes in the human being, Jesus of Nazareth. Only a few recognized him and beheld his true countenance through the human body. These few could do so, because their seeing was supplemented by their trust. Due to their trust, the faith in their hearts, they sensed the Christ in man, Jesus. And when the hour of Golgotha had passed, there were a few in whom the bud of faith opened to the flower of vision. For forty days, they beheld him in their midst. They saw him as if he were a physically visible form, something he no longer was.

Then, forty days later, this special blessing ceased. But the event of Ascension did not signify that the Resurrected One disappeared to human beings. He grew in power and inner strength beyond their faculty of perception. The cloud took him away. The cloud of senses' shine now ruled the souls of the disciples.

In the millennia that have gone by since then, the unseen expansion of the Resurrected One has continued in the periphery of our earth-existence. The Christ sphere has united evermore with the earth-sphere. Eventually, a point in time will come that can be illustrated by a process of nature. When the atmosphere is saturated with moisture, clouds form. In turn, when they are filled with still more moisture, rain falls that wets the ground. A time will come in the Resurrected One's inner development when its living spiritual substance closes in upon the level of human perception. But human consciousness likewise must then have matured. Human souls must become capable of beholding him where, once, the cloud had taken him away. After all, it says, 'He will come even as he departed,' 'He shall come on the clouds of heaven.' Once, he entered *being.* That was the Christmas-event two thousand years ago. Now, he will enter *consciousness,* and this is the Christmas-event intended for our epoch.

*

How do we find the way to that elevation of consciousness which enables us to grow into a discerning touching, a listening hearing and a seeing of that world where the Resurrected One is even now close to us? After all, we are all deeply asleep. The consciousness we possess by virtue of sense perception and rational thinking only concerns a thin surface-layer. The trumpet sounds of our present apocalyptic destiny try to awaken us from this sound sleep. The spirit consciousness that has succumbed to slumber in us is supposed to awaken through the birth-pangs of the tribulations of our age. The world of vision is meant to open to us.

Our dead are likewise in the world into which Christ is coming. At the same time, all of us who unite with the dead whom we love — and who does not have loved departed ones today? — touch that world where Christ draws ever closer to humanity. Today, the departed have this one advantage over the living: even now, they experience the sunrise to which we are still blind. Like the watchman atop the tower, they see the sun while down below we are still surrounded by darkness. A correspondence to this existed in the events two thousand years ago. When, on Good Friday, the Crucified One took his last breath, even then, the light of his sun-nature rose in the domain of the dead that he entered. The light of Easter reached the world of the departed before it arose for human beings on earth. This is the secret of Christ's 'descent to hell.' In our age, it is the same with the new Christmas event. The Christmas light that now is not lyrical but dramatic and apocalyptic, already shines in the realm of our dead. It benefits them, first of all. How does it reach human beings on earth?

Every night, in sleep, we quietly leave our sense world and enter the worlds where our dead are and where the light is shining already. But today we bring so much darkness, dullness and soul-sleep along into the sanctuary of the night that the light does not reach us. When we touch it in deep sleep, we are unable to bring it back into daytime. But we can know that when we are devout and nurture our devotion in community with our dead, then, first during the nights and finally during the day, we will be in a condition to behold the light that shines in the darkness. At Christmas, we always symbolize this by first being in a dark room, then the door opens a little and we see the lights on the Christmas tree. It could happen like this in the dark room of our world today. A door might open just a hair's breath and behind this door the Christmas light shines forth.

The Advent mood, bestowed formerly by nature to human beings when the first snow flakes slowly fell through the air, the first ice flowers glistened on window panes and the stars shone especially brightly in the clear wintry atmosphere, is being extinguished. Let us make it the object of a faithful practice! Let us practice it, and such an opportunity arises wherever an altar stands. To become quiet in front of an altar, to learn the art of devotion, to enliven hope in the soul, a hope that bears its fulfilment within itself through the art of devotion and piety that weave round and enfold this hope, is really like a continuous Advent. But this is an Advent we no longer allow nature to bestow on us. It is one we faithfully plant and interweave into our life according to our own plan. In this domain, penetrating through the trumpet sound of outer destinies, we can then hear God's actual call of love, the harp's sound of Christ's presence.

*

Three steps show us the path that must be traversed. The first step towards beholding that spiritual sun-sphere in which dwells the Christ is to begin to acknowledge the reality of a supersensory world in our thinking. I may only have a faint inkling of such a world, but it is the world that harbours our dead, the one in which Christ is coming to us. It is furthermore the world to which I arise in sleep, the world in which I submerge when I am devout. In a faith-filled thinking that reckons with the reality of God as with the reality of a whole world, a new sense faculty begins to grow. We experience what Luther coined with the word: 'Faith is a new sense extending far beyond the five senses.' Faith turns into an organ of touch; gradually, it becomes more and more natural for us to realize that

what our senses behold is only a mere fraction of the world and
that true existence and destiny lie in that infinite realm that is as
yet concealed to our senses.

The second step consists in learning how to be illuminated and
warmed by this world, even if we cannot yet see it. Just as we
turn to the sun on chilly days to glean a little from its last leave-
taking warmth, so, in the domain of devotion, we can aspire to
the practice of trying to allow ourselves to be reached by the
weaving, wafting element that approaches us from a higher
world. Then, the groping we experience in our thinking is followed by a sort of hearing in our feelings. Through being able
rightly to listen, we begin to touch the sphere where Christ is
behind the words of the Gospel. Here, the prerequisite must be
fulfilled that the Letter to the Hebrews (12:14) expresses in the following way: 'Strive for peace with all men, and for the holiness
without which no one will see the Lord.' Putting this in modern
terms: 'Strive for peace in man and among men and for spiritual-
izing your being. This is the prerequisite for beholding the Lord.'

It is a prophecy proclaimed everywhere in the biblical texts
that it is possible for humans to behold Christ and, in this
beholding, to gain sight of a whole world. The only thing is that,
under the spell of the materialistic world view and the pressure
of a theology that would like to deny the possibility of supersensory perception, these prophecies have not been taken seriously. Let us take a verse from Chapter 1 of the First Letter by
Peter: 'One day Christ will reveal himself to your vision, him
whom you love without having seen him and in whom you
believe even though you do not behold him. Then you will
rejoice with unutterable and exalted joy.' [EB]. When piety qui-
etens the soul and drives out unrest from the human heart, then
an eye opens in the human being that is referred to in the
Beatitudes of the Sermon on the Mount: 'Blessed are the pure in
heart, for they shall see God.' In beholding Christ, they will
acquire vision of God.

The third step is eventually to learn to allow the power of a higher world to stream into our whole will nature. Then Grace is no longer something we passively pray for; it gains entry into us as a new force through our commitment to the will of Christ. How was it for the firstborn of the new vision, for Paul who beheld Christ outside Damascus? Henceforth he could say: 'Not I, but Christ in me.' From this time on, Christ in him was the world-overcoming power that caused him to be active among humanity of that time and allowed effects to be called forth like no other man could bring forth. Yet, it was not he with human power but Christ who worked through him. Not until our will contributes to our relationship with Christ, does it turn into the organ of sight. So long as we only touch the higher sphere with our thinking, we begin with a mere groping. But when we bring our feeling into play, it turns into an inner hearing. When we prepare our will, we learn to open eyes that lead us from faith to sight. This signifies that something higher now reaches into us. Then, Christ is in us; it is really he who illuminates our eye from within in order to behold the light, a light that in turn is *he*. He bears our higher being into us. This brings about forces of the will that allow the scales to fall away from our eyes.

In the First Letter of John (3:3) it says: 'We are God's children and it does not yet appear what we shall be. As yet, our higher being hovers over us. But we know that when it appears we shall be like Him, for we shall see him as he is' [EB]. Our higher being within us turns into an eye, and we behold Christ who is within us, but who is not merely in us but rather is a whole sphere. And it is as if we were looking into a mirror, into an unheard-of mirror of Grace, in which we are allowed to behold, not our earthly being, but our higher nature, which in everyday life is darkened by sin. We behold in this mirror what we are to become one day and what as yet has not appeared. Christ himself is this magical mirror. Paul describes this in the Second Letter to the Corinthians: 'In us is mirrored the Lord's Glory (the Lord's form of light) with unveiled face. And we shall be glorified (meaning, permeated by light) by this light-form from one degree of Glory to another' [EB]. This vision is imminent for humanity and we may steadily ascend into this new Christmas mystery.

The first Christmas event places the image of the *child* before us. The new Christmas event places the image of *man* before us. It is the image of true, whole man who is not merely a fragment, which is what human beings remain if they forget their higher nature. This is why it says that Christ appears in the clouds of heaven as the *Son of Man*. The mirror into which we then may look when our eye ceases to remain in blindness allows us to behold our true goal, our highest goal on earth, the meaning of our life.

The Time Before Christmas

The Christmas announcement, 'Peace on Earth' does not become reality if, somewhere, acts of war simply cease. It is linked to conditions. Not only do the following words contain the qualification: 'to men who are of good will.' Above all, the peace of which the angel spoke to the shepherds presupposes that the divinity in the heights is first made manifest: 'Gloria in Excelsis.' Genuine peace can only exist if something descends into human nature that originates in the heights of the universe. Peace is the condition of a soul that has received the manifesting deity into its being.

We recall the images that filled our souls at Christmas time when we were children, the babe in the manger in Bethlehem. A magical light rays forth from this child as if a sun shone in it. And this splendid mysterious light-source brings it about that, unnoticed by the world, a wondrously ordered configuration comes about. Humanity is grouped around the manger. There are the kings, but likewise the shepherds. There are Joseph and Mary. In the surroundings, as the Christmas plays show us, yet other figures emerge: the hard-hearted innkeepers who do not wish to give shelter to the child, the kind innkeeper who with his lantern guides Mary and Joseph to the stable. But the shadows are not missing either. There are the spectre-like black figures, and in addition Herod who instigates the infanticide. Around the light in the manger arises a design composed of rich and poor, man and woman, old and young, evil and good.

A law becomes evident, similar to one later on when the twelve apostles gathered round the One who had grown up to manhood. They formed a figure that showed that, here, the whole of humanity was represented in all its world-encompassing abundance.

How can the integrating force be explained that proceeded from the light-source in the stable of Bethlehem? High above the earthly, human events that took place in all simplicity, something else simultaneously happened on the world's higher levels of existence. In distant countries, kings who looked up at the stars, became aware that something was about to occur. And the shepherds with their dream-enveloped souls were privileged during this dark night to look at what came to pass in the superphysical realm. They beheld the Glory, the manifesting brightness of the rising spirit-sun above their heads. Around the light formed the circles of all the heavenly hosts. Their harmonious patterns and figures were mirrored below on earth in the humble human groupings. Celestial order rayed down into human existence as the Christ being, the spiritual sun, was revealed and approached in order to enter the earthly world. This is why peace dwelled among human beings of good will, because the order-bestowing sun of revelation shone above the world.

*

Where in our days is the serenity of the manger, the light of Christmas that in earlier times made souls responsive to the magic of the Holy Night? Formerly too, unrest gripped human beings in the weeks before Christmas and it was hard for the stillness of Advent to prevail and cause the depth of soul to become susceptible to the light from on high.

It was the impatience of Advent that drove people to engage in all kinds of busy Christmas preparations. But it was still pervaded by a holy rush, namely the joyful anticipation, the childlike hope for the magic, the cheer of the Christmas celebration. There is a holy rush, the unrest of expectation. Because it was mixed with the unholy rush of human activity, something of the peace-bestowing light of Advent and Christmas time could still shine through. The unrest of expectation was permeated and ensouled by the peace of fulfilment. And not only children, adults likewise dwelled in this atmosphere.

Today, merely unholy rush remains. As good as nothing is left of the once holy excitement of Advent's anticipation, the hope, the expectation of something that was coming. After all, people have no more hope and what they view as hopes are illusions. They cling to calculations that will all be proven wrong. For this reason, to the extent that people do not yield to depression altogether, something of an unholy quiet infuses the bustle of our days. It is the quiet that was experienced when, after the Second World War, one walked through the rubble of Central European cities. It was not merely the stillness of a cemetery, it was the spell that demons of death cast upon the earth, the unrest and silence of doom.

How do we attain holy excitement once more and, through it, sacred serenity which is the prerequisite of the secret of peace? At our altars we can practice something of the mood that opens our soul to peace during the weeks of Advent. There, 'world serenity around us' turns into the element of our life from which divine speech can become audible, speech that bestows harmony and order. But during these weeks of Advent, imbued as they are by the magic of universal quiet, does the sacred ceremony not pose a riddle to us at the same time? Is it not a sharp contradiction to the mood of fulfilled silence, when, of all times, the stern sentences from Chapter 21 of Luke's Gospel resound, sentences that warn of mighty turmoil and upheavals that must come to pass in the world, of disorder even in the forces of heaven, of wars and the cries of battle that will reverberate through the universe? Into the blue colour of the altars during

Advent, in which the secret of 'world serenity around us' becomes a visible experience, the redness of a world-conflagration blends in through the apocalyptic ravages of which the Gospel speaks, ravages that we actually experience today. It becomes evident that the curtain is rent open, that something is trying to manifest; that on the clouds of heaven, in a concealed dimension of existence, he is approaching whose Second Coming shall give the Christmas festival a new content, a new significance.

In our time we have to acquire a sense for what is expiring so as to recognize it and a sense for what is arising so as to nurture it. Outward world conditions are on the verge of decay. To the largest extent possible, the perishable, the temporal is in the process of dying. But the dawn of something new blends into our age as well. And to behold the gently glistening rays of eternity through the tears and cracks of the crumbling sense world gives us the strength calmly to leave the perishable to the abyss and to hold on to what is arising.

In November we still face the unrest of death. November squalls dissolve the old. Along with the yellowed leaves the last remnants of the old year are swirled down to the ground by the gusts of freezing-cold winds. But when the time of Advent begins, one who can look more deeply into nature can become aware of the delicately vibrating excitement of a dawn. The germ, the tiny root of all life in the coming cycle of the year is amove. Now and then, a ray of sunlight shines through the mists and conjures forth a smell that wafts towards us as if coming from a sphere beyond. We sense something for which people in the coming decades will have increasing sensitivity: the etheric world that is hidden behind the curtain of the sensed world. It comes through, it trickles down. Why do we till our gardens and fields before winter arrives? Naturally, one reason is to stimulate the subsequent growth of vegetation from out of the ground. But mainly one does this is so that what comes from the heights can penetrate deeply into the ground, fructifying the earth's life. Human beings walk across the fields and sow the seeds. Invisibly, the heavens sow along with us. This begins during the season of Advent. Heaven sows, even if it causes snow to fall and sends down the freezing cold. A farmer knows that the more the ground freezes, the more fertile it will be.

At this point one would like to change directions as happens in the ancient Christmas plays when the star-singer says:

> Dear singers mine, think otherwise,
> To greet the *star*, let us arise.

During Advent-time we have to learn to greet the star. When the haze of the old year has lifted completely, space is open, the atmosphere is purified and stars begin to stream down into our earthly existence. With the starry forces, heaven sows new life into earth's womb. Do the snow flakes not have starry shapes? The weeks of Advent are Mother Earth's time of conception. And at Christmas, Earth becomes Mary and delivers her child. Within earth's innermost depths, a seed of light is engendered by the stars. Earth's inmost depths become the manger in which a little child sends out light. It gets up so as to arise. The manger, too, in the earth's womb is surrounded by compositions and figures, just as they were modestly indicated in Bethlehem in shepherds and kings, Mary and Joseph, lastly in oxen and the donkey that stood nearby so as to receive something of the new light. All round in the arising circle dwell the stars like in twelve chambers, the stars that come to visit earth at his season. This is why folklore relates that during the holy nights all the flowers that will sprout forth in spring move their little heads and ring their bells in the earth's womb. Why do so many flowers have the forms of stars? Because the stars enter earth in winter's night. Down below, the shapes of plant and flower existence are already present supersensibly. In spring, they become visible to our senses as well.

The moment when the child of new life is born in earth's depths is significant. Truth it is that the twelve nights that follow Holy Night harbour a mystery. During this time, it is as if the infant had risen from his manger and were beginning to climb up; he moves upwards as in a circular stairway in a tower and passes by the chambers in which dwell the stars' forces. Thus, what will unfold in the twelve months of the new year is prepared during the holy nights between Christmas and Three Kings Day. The stars are made manifest out of the heights and in the depths of earth a sacred order comes about. The peace they initiate wafts towards us from the plant kingdom's paradisal radiance that refreshes us evermore.

What we can learn from it is this: we must start quite far down at the bottom when we wish to tread an inner path, even as earth begins deep down below when bringing forth new life. We will hang in mid-air throughout our life if we do not start deep within. Profound concentration, quiet and devotion are required for this. Only in the manger of his innermost being can man turn into Mary and receive the essential Christmas gift. What people commonly receive as presents at Christmas can all too easily divert our minds from the actual gifts of the Holy Night that stream towards us from the stars' cornucopia, from the etheric world through the special quality of wintry nature. Every night when the stars sparkle brightly, but likewise when clouds cover them, the air is filled with revelation. During the night of nights, we can open our soul for it like at no other time. Then peace moves into our hearts, peace promised by the Christmas proclamation.

*

For two thousand years, Christ is intimately connected with the earth's breath that experiences such a wondrous new beginning at the time of the winter solstice. Along with the seed of light that is born there in the earth's core, Christ himself rises up in the twelve nights of the Christmas season. This has been forgotten long since. But now we may once again experience Christianity in the cosmic sense. We may know: by experiencing the seasons of the year rightly, particularly where the year's cycle is born anew out of the primal nadir of existence, we approach the sphere of the present-day Christ, for he dwells in the etheric world. This etheric world is proclaimed at Advent time all the way even to our senses. All the meaningful customs of placing Christmas trees in our homes and lighting candles on them originate from pagan, cosmic intimations by Northern European folk streams that were still capable of perceiving and accompanying the spiritual element in nature. Here, without really admitting it, a union was concluded early on between Christian and pagan inclinations. Against the cosmic power of the Christmas festival, the Church could not maintain the barrier it had erected against all other pagan influences.

Even though the ancient magic moods of Christmas have been lost to us, it is still proper to pass through Advent and Christmas time with the awareness that something quite special is taking place in the course of the year. By living with the renewed ritual of the Christian Community we have once again begun to sense the significance of consecration. What does it mean when people or objects are consecrated? It means that they are lifted back up to their spiritual origin, their archetypal condition, the state they were in before they were solidified out of spirit into matter. The primal spiritual state of all existence, that which is akin to a fresh spring of water, to the very young and to the Christ-childlike element in all and everything, this is called forth out of concealment through proper acts of consecration. The sentence that this or that 'is put in order again' presupposes that order was originally inherent in all existence, order that came from the stars. On earth, this starry order is lost. If it does not pass into chaos and dissolution, it is buried.

The actual meaning of the Act of the Consecration of Man is that it straightens human beings out inasmuch as it unveils their archetype, Man as conceived by God. The higher being of man that originates in the spirit descends to our soul. Ultimately, this is the peace that arises in us when we gather around the altar in devotion. It is the peace that is addressed when those who have participated in Communion receive the greeting of peace. And even as human beings receive a consecration through the Sacrament, the whole year, the whole earth, receives a conse-cration purely through the priestly element of all-bountiful nature during the Holy Night. In Earth's womb, the configura-tions that stars carry within come alive again, configurations that were lost in earth-existence. Oh, if human beings would only take up these configurations, shining forth as they do at Christmas-time, and would structure civilization accordingly instead of basing it on empty expediencies that merely become reduced to absurdity! At Christmas-time, the longing should at least be present to create replicas of the starry order on earth, to allow the cosmic element to irradiate the earthly realm. The three Christmas Acts of Consecration are a primal consecration. They glean man's consecration from earth's consecration. At the year's midnight hour, the sacred vessels are filled anew out of starry heights. All the troubles and decay notwithstanding, something will in time come to life again of what people for-merly linked to December 24, once called Adam and Eve Day. For paradise will be present again. The primal state, the spirit origin of our earth-existence will once more be tangibly close to us and we will draw from it as from the holiest of wellsprings.

*

In this way, the new content of Christmas becomes familiar to us. We can no longer be sustained by looking back to the Christmas event two thousand years ago. Then, Christ ap-

peared in human form. The birth of Christ was physically localized. Only where Jesus of Nazareth moved about could Christ
be directly perceived by human beings. The opposing powers
were likewise physically localized when, on the Isle of Capri,
Tiberius in his Caesarean madness became the instrument of demonic powers. Today, Christ approaches earth anew, but not in
such a form that one could say, he is here or there. Neither will
it be possible to say of the Antichrist, he is or was this or that
person. Today, light and shadow are omnipresent, because
overall a new effect of super- sensory world is coming upon us.
The sphere of the spiritual world closest to our sense world, the
realm of the ether forces, must be discovered by human beings.
For in it, the new Christmas event takes place. There, Christ is
even now present. We just do not see him yet, because our eyes
have not yet opened for it.

In the words in which Christ himself speaks of his return, he
indicates that at his Second Coming the configurations of the
heavenly hosts around him will be present and effective: 'But
when the Son of man will come on the clouds of heaven in all
his glory and all his holy angels with him, then will the world
of earthly tribes gather round him' (Rev.1:7 EB). This is what
basically is occuring now behind the veils of the sense world.
The whole supersensory world is gathered before our portals.
The central light within it is the Christ-entity and in a surrounding circle are the stars of all the leading spirit-powers.
When this living sphere of existence is mirrored in our earthly
life, then order and peace will prevail among human beings.
This need not be identical with external political order and
outer peace. The peace of the future must be found even in the
midst of the discord of war.

On earth, order does not reign, only chaos. Why? In an external sense, the world has developed at headlong speed, particularly in technology, and inwardly human beings have not kept
pace. The consequence is that everything collapses. Chaos is the

result of the fact that we were outwardly active without pos-
sessing the gold value of inwardness. When the events taking
place in our time behind the veil of cloud-existence in the
Christ-sphere can be reflected in human life, then only can new
orders and configurations shine forth. Secrets of numbers are
fulfilled that are indicated in John's Revelations where mention
is made of the hundred and forty-four thousand. Once human
beings evolve and mature beyond the gaping abysses of hatred
to the point of allowing the configurations of star-existence and
the hierarchical Christ-circumference to enter in upon them,
then, from among all the nations, communities will form that
are not based on blood ties. Above the separate nations, in the
order-bearing archetype, stands the number twelve, twelve
thousand, which in this expanded form signifies the community. Nations, too, are arranged in a circle of twelve in the sphere
of the archetypal images, a circle that, even as does the circle of
the twelve Apostles, represents the whole of humanity. This is
how the number twelve times twelve thousand — 144,000 —
spiritually comes into being. But this number will yet slumber
for a long time as a secret within mankind. It is the number of
peace, of harmony between the polarities. Quantitatively, these
communities, where something of these archetypes and prom-
ises will be fulfilled, may well be quite small. But in this way,
the 'Peace on Earth' will begin to unfold as a reflection of what
is revealed in the heights.

The Midnight Hour of the Year

In earlier times people knew that midnight is the witching-hour. They tried to be asleep or at least to be under the protective roof of their home when the clock struck twelve, or else they feared they might encounter the evil one

Did escape into sleep really occur only for negative reasons? Did one merely try to evade the ghostly shiver of the earthly witching-hour? Was one not attracted by the mystery of support and blessings that approached the soul from the depth of sleep particularly in the 'middle of the night'? If, to this day, it is said that the sleep before midnight is the best sleep, then this originally did not only mean that it provided the most physically refreshing sleep. Rather, it meant that the soul of the sleeping person could drink most deeply from the heavenly spheres' fountain of youth. For those who sleep, there must exist a blessed spirit-hour, of which the earthly witching-hour is merely a frightening, spectral shadow and counter-image.

*

Sleep is a brother to death. It carries the soul on its wings to the same spheres into which the soul-spiritual being of man gradually ascends when it has passed through the gate of death. Here, the modern Copernican world view, of which humanity is so proud, does not count, for it only applies to the physical and

material exterior of the world. The world of sleeping human beings and the departed follows the configurations of the ancient
Ptolemaic world view. This view could be scorned and declared
outdated only when people no longer understood that it does
not relate to the world of physical incarnation but to that of the
existence before birth and after death, to a body-free existence
in soul- and spirit-land.

In space, where Earth is enveloped by the mantle of air, the
atmosphere, it is enveloped in the super-spatial, spiritual sense
by the seven spheres, of which Moon, Mercury, Venus, Sun,
Mars, Jupiter and Saturn with their celestial orbits are merely
spatial indications of borders.

All genuine descriptions of what human beings have to
undergo on yonder side of the portal of death — be they
mythological descriptions that originate from ancient vision or
from present-day spiritual research expressed in thought-
forms — indicate that entry and passage through the central
one of the seven spheres, the sun-sphere, is decisive for the
structure of evolving future human destiny. Until then, the
human being had to pass through the stages of purification. All
the impure, incomplete elements lacking goodness that they
carried along from earthy life, had to be left behind in the three
lower spheres, those of the soul-land. It may be that not much
has remained of a human being when the entrance to the centre of the universe is approached. Here, 'the sun' reveals the
actually indestructible fruit of the earth-life that has ended.
Dimming night has befallen the largest part of the human
being. At the border of soul- and spirit-land the human being
enters the sphere of the cosmic midnight-hour, and — paradoxical as it may appear to earthly thinking — this is the sun
sphere. The part of us that passes the test is privileged at this
decisive threshold to behold 'the sun at midnight' on its journey through the spheres of life after death. The Sun, beheld at
the centre of the universe is the fountain out of which the

human entity receives the mighty rejuvenation, the strength for building up its future destiny.

*

If sleep at night is what it really should be, meaning, if by the way we spend our waking hours, we do not absorb so much ballast that it lames our soul's wings during the night, then sleep will lift us up through the same spherical stages in shortened, compressed sequence. It will moreover have its midnighthour, in which it bears us into the sun-centre of the universe. In more ancient, childlike times, the inner midnight-hour of sleep still coincided with the earthly time of midnight. But sleep can even lead modern human beings, who only too frequently have to turn night into day, to the 'sun at midnight.' Borne by angels, the soul passes through the fountainhead of creation where, in spirit spheres, the cosmic Word perpetually voices the command: 'Let there be light!' Only the sun of night-time refreshes and revitalizes sleep in the deepest sense so much that waking up in the morning turns into something like being born anew. Without it, we do not bring the sunny state of a rejuvenated heart and mind out of the nocturnal fount of youth that lights up the day from within for us. A typically modern person has forfeited the cosmic depth of sleep. We remain without the sun's blessing of night and, even if we devote a sufficient number of hours to resting at night, we go on our way tired, spent and depressed. Instead of being a guest of the celestial spirit-hour, we become a victim of the earthly witching-hour that former generations eluded in their sleep. Because our soul does not reach up at night to the high sphere of the spiritual sun, during the day it likewise lacks wings for soaring flight of genius. Because the sun does not illuminate midnight for us, night-apparitions darken our sun-radiant day.

*

Once in the course of the year, the mystery of the 'sun at the midnight-hour,' which otherwise is reserved for the super-spatial spheres of heaven, touches upon our physical, earthly world. The blessings of the spiritual sun fully descend to earth once in nature's rhythmical course. This occurs at the winter solstice when the outward sun's physical effects of light and warmth have receded to the greatest extent. It is as if the physical sun has then withdrawn farthest from earth; night here on the earth has reached its greatest ascending over daytime; it is the midnight-hour of the year. But it is for the sake of earth that the physical sun withdraws. This happens so that the sun likewise can approach the fountainhead of cosmic life and from it renew its forces for the life-producing activity of sending its rays into the new year's cycle. In the cosmic Bethlehem of 'spirit-land,' namely the spiritual sun-sphere, the earthly sun is newly born at the winter solstice. 'In the midst of winter's cold, half through the night,' the sun himself is the light-filled babe in the manger of heaven that lights up the dark cave of all darkness. The nascent state, the very first primal and powerful growth of the newborn sun of the coming year is the secret of the thirteen 'holy nights between the years,' particularly the Holy Night that initiates this elevated span of time. The physical sun relinquishes its space and course so that the celestial spirit-hour of the 'sun at the midnight hour' can pour its restorative sovereign power not only into these nights but even into physical waking life, driving away the spectres of the terrestrial witching hour.

When, in the little town of Bethlehem, far from the noisy throng of people, in the rocky grotto that served as a stable, the Jesus child was born and, like a shining sun, illuminated the darkness that surrounded the manger, there arose a pure human replica of the cosmic sun-mystery that was fulfilled during the same hour of the year. The holy night of worlds turned into the earth's holy-night-event. In the shepherds asleep in the

fields, there lived the 'seeing of the sun at midnight' in con-
summate soul-power in such a way that they became aware of
how the cosmic mystery providentially coincided with the birth
on earth of the longed-for Messiah. With the stream of sacramental life, we follow the creative, spiritual and physical course
of the sun in the year's midnight-hour, when we celebrate the
Christmas festival with the three Acts of the Consecration of
Man that begin on Christmas Eve at midnight and lead on to
Christmas Day. Thus, the 'sun at midnight' likewise becomes
the source from which the sacramental stream is newly sustained for a coming year, when for those of us who kneel at the
manger in Bethlehem, the window opens at midnight towards
the cosmic Bethlehem into which, at other times, the angels only
bear body-free sleeping and departed souls in spirit-land.

Today, the world is midnight-like in the sense of the spectral
earthly witching-hour. One need not wait for the hour at
midnight to encounter evil. Those who know of the Christmas-
aspect of midnight and each year deeply take to heart the spirit-
hour of Christ when the sun becomes visible in the cosmic
Bethlehem through the image of the babe in the manger, can
help carry the light of Christmas into outward midnight-
darkness.

The New Year in
the Light of Epiphany

As expressed in the name of the month, January, the turn of the year in the middle between Christmas and Epiphany always has the Janus-head with the two faces, the one that looks back and the other that looks forward. What did the past year bring and what will be brought by the new year? What outer and inner challenges develop for us from past events and achievements for the new year and the time that lies ahead?

We should look forward without fear and with inner readiness even for hardships to what the new year will bring *outwardly*. What it will bring *inwardly* depends on us. Will we make inner advances that will hold the balance against possible external advances, inner advances that afterwards will furthermore constitute the blessing inherent in endured sorrow?

One might raise the doubt-filled question whether it is even possible to know anything about what the new year will bring. But it is quite possible to know what it will bring if humanity simply continues to plunge still more deeply into materialism and allows the last connections with the higher worlds to be severed. But all this not withstanding, we can be aware above all of what is taking place above our heads, for it is indeed happening even now and awaits the possibility of unfolding higher forces. Black clouds darken our sight, reflecting our merely earth-bound efforts. But the events of Salvation that occur

above the clouds are likewise recognizable. It is quite possible
to develop prophetic, apocalyptic awareness and knowledge in
looking up to this sphere and in this way to acquire certitude
in the face of life's growing difficulties. Among all the soul-
spiritual capacities that abounded in the congregations in the
days of early Christendom, the Apostle Paul primarily wanted
to see that the gift of prophecy was cultivated. In the congregations, more than speaking in tongues and even healing, nurturing the gift of prophecy, the talent of apocalyptic knowledge
of what takes place above our heads was important to him.
This consciousness was to be enkindled from looking up to the
light that had arisen for him at Damascus. This admonition by
the apostle probably applies to us today even more than to the
early Christian communities. We need not go forward blindly
into the future with eyes closed. If one resolution for the new
year is justified, it is the one that we reinforce each other in the
awareness that Christ is present, that he has entered into a new
proximity to humanity through his coming on the clouds.
Christ, the present one, the forevermore Coming One — this
has to be fundamental to our faith especially in each newly
beginning year.

*

New Year's Eve is not just a matter of the date in an arbitrary
calendar. It is the middle of the thirteen Holy Nights and thus
truly the balancing point of Christmas time, a time that extends
from the night of the Shepherds to the day of the Kings. And
Christmas time is probably the most instructional time in the
year's course. The actual Christmas festival still belongs in the
old year. At the end of the Christmas-octave comes the festival
of Epiphany which belongs in the new year. Properly speaking,
Christmas looks backward, Epiphany looks forward. We have
to participate inwardly in the turn from the retrospective view

to the one directed to the future. Then the thought of Epiphany can help us best to enter into an apocalyptic attitude for the year that has newly begun.

At Christmas, we recall the birth of the human being, Jesus. In him, the quintessence of all human history was present, the reason why the gospels place such great value on the genealogies. The noblest that could mature from mankind's history had become man in Jesus of Nazareth, one who from his previous earth-destinies bore in himself the inmost fruits of all cultures.* And if we do not merely look at Matthew's Nativity story but likewise at the one in the third Gospel, we have to say: through Luke's Christmas-child, the quintessence of all the heavens' history, of what in distant past ages took place above the heads of earthly men has entered earth's course. For here we deal with an entity that came directly out of paradise, a being that preserved the paradisal legacy during all the directions on which humanity had to travel deeper and deeper into the earthly realm. Christmas allows us to look into the past; it places before us sacred human figures in whom all the past times become humanized and incarnated. Epiphany, on the other hand, relates to the birth of Christ even as Christmas does to the birth of Jesus. And we only grasp the Christ being when we understand that all future time is contained in him. He *is* everlasting future. He is that divine entity in the universe whose very nature is that of ever growing and becoming, never that of having become, even if we see Christ in the Gospel in scenes that, to us, seem to be in the past. In all the scenes of the Gospel, we must move on from the Jesus-aspect to the Christ-aspect in order, therein, to discover the ever-present future.

Epiphany means 'light-appearance from above.' This is why the festival of Epiphany is called the 'Festival of Appearance' in

* See details in E. Bock, *The Childhood of Jesus*, Floris Books.

some regions. Even this shows that January 6 is not simply Three Kings' Day. Stars always appear in the heavens; the star whom the kings followed must have special significance. Behind it, an epiphany must be concealed. It is the ongoing epiphany, meaning, the ongoing light-revelation from above that became manifest, as it were, for the first time on that date. And according to Christian tradition, it was indeed customary to celebrate the adoration of the three kings as well as to remember how Jesus was baptized thirty years later by John the Baptist on January 6. The dual aspects of this date make it evident that not merely one historical moment is being indicated. Inasmuch as another instance is included that occurred thirty years later, we experience a living forward movement. The tension between the two festive contents draw us into the stream of forward-moving time.

But what was the star of the Magi? It is a profound misunderstanding, an attempt at comprehension on far too low a level, if we assume that the three Magi from the East were astrologers and simply observed a special constellation in the sky, as birth horoscope, as it were, of the boy referred to in the Gospel of Matthew. This may have played a secondary role, for, naturally, the stars stood in a special position when a human being such as Jesus of Nazareth was born. But something else is meant by the star whom the three kings followed. Something else is referred to when we are told that this star moved like a guide in front of the three kings. A star really does not do this, but this star did. Here, a passage from a lecture by Rudolf Steiner can help us gain more insight. He spoke of Three Kings' Day. He described the three kings from the East as initiates who, with their power of seership that reached across land and sea, hence beyond spatial dimensions could focus on soul-spiritual facts:

To be led by a star means that the soul itself is viewed as a star. One beholds the soul as a star if one can beholds it as a radiant aura ... What illuminated the Magi's path was none other than the soul of Christ.*

When such insights, originating as they do from a new form of clairvoyant research, are correctly understood, it signifies that, in those days in various regions of the Orient, initiated men directed their inner vision to a particular soul, namely, the most advanced human soul that was on the verge of incarnating on earth as a human being. And, transcending all spatial distances, as they clairvoyantly beheld how the soul of this human being was moving towards birth, they became aware that a greater light-source poured into this soul in an epiphany from above. They therefore not only beheld the birth of a human child, rather, they realized: when this man will have grown up, the great, leading aura, the soul of Christ himself, will enter him. Understood in this way, the vision beheld by the three kings was a prophetic experience in two ways. They not only envisioned the birth of a human being; they looked further into the future and became aware what sort of epiphany would one day be fulfilled for this man. This is the reason why Three Kings' Day is likewise called the Day of Epiphany. It was not just a star that shone in the heavens. It was the Guiding Spirit throughout all of humanity's history that manifested to these initiates. Thus, travelling on separate routes, they could finally arrive at the place where the little boy was born who was over-shadowed by his Christ-future.

In the same lecture by Rudolf Steiner, we find the indication that January 6 was an important religious festival among many people of the ancient world, namely, the Festival of Osiris. The myth of the twilight of the gods was summed up in the name of Osiris. It relates how the sun-genius Osiris was torn to pieces by his sinister opponent Typhon and how a piece of him is buried in every individual human being. But the people of antiquity

* Lecture of December 30, 1924.

had the certainty that, some time in the future, Osiris would arise again. This would be when the star of love, which as yet was still shining in the higher worlds, would come down to earth so that all earthly passions of human beings would receive the stamp of nobility through heavenly love. One can therefore say: the three kings from the Orient saw that fulfilment was imminent of what had ensouled them in their Osiris-festival as Messianic hope and expectation.

*

The appearance of the star referred to by the Matthew Gospel is truly an epiphany, a present but at the same time prophetic happening. The bearer of an ongoing sun-revelation, of an epiphany that asserted itself, emerged in the environment of the earth. During the Baptism in the Jordan, thirty years after that day of the three kings, the 'star,' that is, what stood as a mighty epiphany behind the star, would move into the human being, Jesus of Nazareth. This was experienced likewise by John the Baptist, of whom it says in the Gospel of John that heaven opened to him and that he looked into the opened heaven at the moment when he baptized Jesus. This, however, is only the first fulfilment of the star-prophecy. One can say: when the star appeared, it was the beginning of the apocalypse. The three kings were the first apocalyptists. In the Christ-future, they beheld the Messianic fulfilment that would not come all at once but would become reality among humanity through the mighty steps of sacred evolution.

In the three years, the 'star' unfolded. We might call to mind the moment when the three apostles were on Mount Tabor together with Jesus. All at once, the radiant light of the Christ being shone forth from the human figure of Jesus, and all earthly matter was transfigured in this light. There, the epiphany progressed further. And it advanced still further in the events

following Easter, when the Resurrected One sent out the disciples, and yet further until the event of Whitsun. Here it became
evident that the 'star' could lead. The star's powerful leadership became manifest in the apostolic mission, which, as if from
within, caused the apostles to journey throughout the lands.
The star did not merely guide the kings, it led the apostles when
they went out into the world to proclaim the Gospel.

It is an epiphany-course that the New Testament follows
from the gospels which look back to what happened two thousand years ago all the way to John's Revelation that look forward to the future of humanity and earth. The Letters of Paul
that lie between belong in a sense to the Apocalypse. Even
though Paul knows the retrospective element, vision of the
future is more important to him. In the noon-hour at Damascus,
the epiphany moved forward for him. Damascus was a mighty,
prophetic anticipation of mankind's future. Paul experienced
the new light of epiphany as a precursor, a forerunner of a
humanity that, starting in our time, is to find its Damascus. And
even if, initially, there are only a few from whose eyes the scales
fall, it is only in this way that humanity will find its rightful way
towards the future.

Finally, there is Patmos, where the mighty Apocalypse was
received by the soul and spirit of the Apostle John. This is a further stage of the Epiphany. Here, the 'star' is the guide through
the evolution of the world from one aeon to the next.

The great future perspective unfolds: the seven seals are
opened, the seven trumpets resound and the seven golden
bowls are poured out. For us, the Apocalypse is the guideline of
prophetic power in the soul.

It can become a very real New Year's impulse to remember
that Epiphany leads from the Christmas star to Christ's Second
Coming. The course of life of the human being, Jesus of
Nazareth, was confined to thirty-three years. The Christ's
course of life only began then and moves on from one epiphany

to the next, from one clarity to the next. If, in our time, the Christmas mood of yester-year is difficult to evoke, we need not mourn it. Is it not understandable that the Christmas mood, which originates from looking back to an event of the past, pales when he, who emerged only then as a star over humanity, is once again here? Today, humankind must find its way from a Christmas past to a Christmas of the future, to an apocalyptic Christmas festival. Even today, one must still think of the Christmas that took place in the earthly realm in Bethlehem in Palestine. But above all, we today require the outlook on humanity as a whole. Since the beginning of the twentieth century, Christ is here again. And what takes place above our heads is the unfolding of the Christmas star in the present, the great epiphany of Christ's new presence, of his nascent Second Coming. We stand in the very midst of the dynamic future. Even now, the future is reality all around us. We can read in the books of the future by cultivating an apocalyptic, prophetic awareness and thus live towards what is coming. Even Paul designates the mighty humanity-enveloping Damascus-light, the *parousia*, the Second Coming of Christ, as the Epiphany. He encourages his disciple and helper, Timothy, to do his utmost in order to experience the epiphany himself and encounter Christ in the spirit. In saying so, he uses the very instructive expression of the 'individual times.' He who is coming comes not according to a calendar at such and such a date. He comes at individual times; for any one individual when the hour is right:

Exert all your inner power until the appearance (the epiphany) of our Lord Jesus Christ, (the epiphany), which, in each case at the individual times, will be made manifest by the Blessed and only Sovereign, the King of kings and Lord of all lords, who alone has immortality and dwells in unapproachable light, whom no man has ever seen or can see; to him be honour and eternal dominion. (1Tim.6:14-16 EB)

The Battle of Life with Death

The content of Holy Week is composed of the encounter between death and life. What does the contrast between the Cross
on Golgotha and the life bursting from all vegetation try to tell
us? Where does the Cross stand today that stood two thousand
years ago on Golgotha? Then, human beings crucified a god because they did not recognize him. Today, humanity recognizes
the divine even less than they did then and therefore crucifies it
even more. But today's humanity not only fails to recognize the
divine, it even misunderstands the secret of life. In the First
Letter to the Corinthians, Paul says concerning the divine glory:
'If the rulers of this world had recognized this glory, they would
not have crucified the Lord of glory.' (1Cor.2:8 EB) Today, one
would have to say: since human beings no longer understand
the secret of life, they nail life and the Lord of life onto the cross
of death everywhere.

Actually, what is life? When winter slowly yields to the
warming light of spring, the magic of life manifests in the tender green hue that suffuses the dead-looking world. Then the
buds grow and spring forth quickly under the waxing sun and
the spring rains. Creatively, they produce an immeasurable
wealth of green foliage, blooming flowers and bountiful fruits.
Nobody can explain this miracle with the ideas that presently
prevail in science. At most, one can describe it. We have long
since become so accustomed to it that we no longer notice our
incomprehension. We have developed thought-forms that only

grasp the inanimate, because we merely move along physical matter. In the end, we even believe that the secret of life could be derived from matter. In reality, another world extends into the realm of matter. Life is the lowest level of the supersensory world which in its totality, including the highest divine spheres, has slipped from human consciousness. It is no surprise that human beings do not really know how to value life. Since they do not recognize it, they waste it and lose it. They nail the life of the world and their own on the cross of matter. Thus, Golgotha is ever present among us, and it is part of a modern human being's proper awareness of Holy Week to draw a 'balance of life.' When we observe the quantity of life available to us on our planet Earth, we make the shocking discovery that it is declining significantly. We confront such a deficit of life that it can never again be covered. The planet is caught up in a dying process of the greatest possible dimensions and this is man's doing. With all the triumphs of the human spirit we have basically brought on an immense, wholesale death. The holocausts of the recent past are not even the only aspects. In the animal and plant kingdoms, a no less disturbing degree of mass-dying takes place. Machines are conquering space that until now was occupied by living beings. Dead instruments supplant living entities. Animal species without number are on the verge of extinction. All the continents are in the grip of an incalculable transformation of woodland into steppe, because people believe they can sustain life by mechanical methods, through drainage of the ground, with chemically produced fertilizers and other means of death. With these methods, we can only reduce the sum of life on earth even more.

Valuation of human life has reached an appalling form. During the years of World War Two, the true state of affairs became evident on occasion. Call to mind the horrific instances, when the corpses of those who had been murdered in the concentration camps of horror were thrown onto a heap, and the victims were frequently checked only for gold fillings in their mouth or a gold ring on their finger. Indeed, many far more brutal considerations existed that measured living beings merely by their crude material value. Under numerous disguises and pretences, this way of thinking has continued in many areas.

*

To the *obvious* death that becomes visible in the genocide of modern wars and the countless victims of modern traffic, a masked death is added that has made inroads in the living human being and seizes upon one soul province after the other. This death tries to turn human beings into corpses while still alive, into a withered, unfeeling, loveless statistician of world events, into a cog of the machine of utilitarianism. If it becomes important nowadays to learn to distinguish between different states of mind, this may no longer relate only to the discrimination between good and evil, meaning between angels and demons. This skill begins where it is a matter of distinguishing between what is alive and what is dead. We all think that it goes without saying that we can do that. But that is a dangerous delusion. When we explore the spirituality that is at work in a person, the standard we have to apply is whether it is a spirituality that augments life or one that increases death. Presently, a spirituality dominates throughout that nowhere can produce anything living and therefore remains in the service of death.

But is thinking something dead? Can we not record the most astounding triumphs of the human spirit? Certainly, but don't most new inventions serve to destroy and kill more efficiently? Basically, all these 'new ideas' point in one direction. During the final phase of the mighty catastrophes of the Second World War, there were moments when people believed that quite novel means of warfare, quite new strategic ideas would be put to use. In reality, these were not new ideas, only a consistent progression of thinking in mechanical logic which had previously existed. People simply let go of the last compunctions they had still maintained in regard to God and human beings. It no longer made a difference if one dealt with human beings. 'Total war' came into vogue inasmuch as warfare was mechanized without restraint. War was to run its course like a huge mechanism. In essence, this is the appearance of all the present-day achievements of the human spirit. Modern humans do not produce life-giving, productive, creative ideas. People can be clever, they can make the most unheard-of inventions, but they do not do it by means of creative thoughts. They do it because they allow the machine, the system to think. Even what is termed 'organization' is in most cases the cogency of the system and leads to increased bureaucracy of all life. While one would like to decrease the number of officials, the system does not permit it and its structure grows immeasurably. Once mechanical principles are allowed into the garden of life, they cannot easily be controlled again.

Naturally, the results of calculating thoughts to which labour and life are directed nowadays cannot simply be declared ineffective. But it should be realized that the spirit only seemingly intervenes creatively in the world of matter. The thinking that prevails today does not belong among man's actual *inner* accomplishments. Rather, it must be counted among man's most *external* activities. Thinking that takes its course merely in the inert, grey matter of the brain, is only apparently alive. In reality, there thinks death. A spirituality of death that is hostile to life proceeds from there. People produce useful objects, substances and devices by dismantling and disintegrating matter and putting it back together in a different manner. But all this is a great display of transience and death. When, in our days, the analysis of matter progresses so far that the realm of atomic energy is reached, one does find spirituality, but it is the spirituality of death in its ultimate exposure. The true spirit-opposing demon rises in eerie ghostly dimensions out of the abyss. And if a newspaper headline reads: 'Atomic Energy: Givers of Life or Rays of Death?' one wonders: has somebody perhaps realized what this is all about? But here, accurate insights will arise only when it is recognized what 'life' actually is. We cannot know what life is so long as we remain caught up in materialism and deny the existence of the supersensory world of which the lowest sphere is that of life.

*

Humanity as a whole had to approach a cosmic position of Passion Week. We have reached it today. We have arrived at our Golgotha, the human spirit's Place of the Skull. Here is the end of all natural life: the cross, the sign of death, rises up. And even as Good Friday was followed two thousand years ago by Holy Saturday, which held the secret of Christ's Descent into Hell, so we today have approached the human spirit's descent to hell. Out of the abyss, the ominous swarm of cold demonic forces fumes upward, unleashed by human beings themselves through their soulless thoughts. The fourth seal of John's Revelation shows us today's Good Friday image: death riding on the pale horse and hell, Hades, following him.

The biblical saying, 'The wage of sin is death' can illuminate the apocalyptic life-deficit of our age as an ultra-modern saying. But these words do not refer to sin committed by an individual, but to sin as the condition of humanity that have fallen into farthest distances from God. To this belongs the Fall of knowledge in particular, due to which human beings have arrived at dead thinking. The wage of this sin can only be a general spell of death that is imposed on earth and mankind.

When, two thousand years ago, Good Friday's darkness and earthquake were over, spectral appearances of the dead were observed in Jerusalem that frightened people. Something had to have happened in the realm of the dead, but one did not know what it was. Then, on Easter morn, at least a few found the solution after the fact. They realized that something had truly happened in the world of the dead. A being had entered this realm, over whom death had no power, One who confronted death as the victor. It was the Lord of Life who had brought this movement into the world of the departed; he had caused the Descent into Hell to follow the hour of Golgotha.

Why do so many mysterious supersensory inklings and appearances flicker and flash through our world? Has something perhaps happened again in the realm of the dead into which so many millions of souls had to enter due to the turbulence of the age? Is another Easter possibly drawing near again through which it becomes clear that it is once again the Lord of Life who brings movement into the world of the dead? The first Easter morning was the belated key for all the puzzling agitation. The Damascus-event that lights up among human beings here and there will after the fact illuminate and shed light on all the results and riddles of our age.

*

How do we find the transition from the human spirit's Golgotha and descent into hell, in which we find ourselves now, to a resurrection and ascension of man's spirit?

Christ's Resurrection is not simply one momentary event that took place on Easter morn. As 'the victory over death,' it was the conclusion of a battle that ran through Christ's whole life. With what kind of weapon and power did he wage this battle? In him dwelled the glowing fire-power of inner keenness and activity. It arose in him in this form at the moment of the Baptism in the Jordan and for three years battled against the forces of death. Life itself manifested in this inner activity with unique might and finally vanquished death's strength. The fire-related inner activity was expressed as sovereignty of spirit over matter. Only one word had to be spoken to a human being or a hand laid on a sick person, and streams of life poured forth. A constant priestly service took place, albeit without an external altar. The whole human life of Christ was a sacramental process. His nature was like an ongoing prayer and sacrificial flame. From here we can understand what happened on the eve of Maundy Thursday when he gave bread and wine to the disciples and said: this is my body, this is my blood. The spirit's sovereignty of transubstantiation over matter manifested. Here, the spirit of death that unleashes the nether world's spirit-element in matter no longer ruled;. no, the super-earthly spiritual element of life penetrated and transformed matter.

Can we quicken something in us of this inner activity that attains victory over dying and death? We must admit in all honesty how weak our souls are. The profusion of external activities has increased so much in our time that an inner activity can hardly prevail against it. Life runs its course like a movie for a modern human being. We no longer make an actual effort to exert any influence on this, and even less, the more outer assiduity and activity we develop in the external sense. We do not come to be ourselves because we do not find the inner composure that is the prerequisite for any inner activity. The inner being at most stirs under the influence of a hard blow of fate or perhaps a particularly happy occasion. Maybe it is aroused now and then among poets, musicians, sculptures and musicians — last vestiges of the life-provision under the depression of death. The minimum of inner activity that has been reached by humanity today represents the actual distance of our age from Christ. We can call ourselves Christians; but if we do not have anything of this inner activity, we are not Christians. He who merely participates in the unrecognized magic of death in external activities and does not counter them with something of the fire of inner keenness of mind, can be a Christian in name only.

*

How do we reach the point of developing the inner drive that leads to the spirit of life, not that of death? Above all, it is important to liberate our thinking, which has reached its Calvary, from the spell of crucifixion. If it learns to unite again with reverence, it will tear itself free of the tyranny of being fettered to the brain. It ceases to be mere cold cleverness. Thinking will be linked once again with thankfulness and devotion. The heart must learn to think along with the head. Then a thinking arises in which inner activity is once more contained. Rudolf Steiner has described it in his *Philosophy of Freedom* and many other books. The creative principle flames up again in the human spirit; living spirit soars upward beyond the mere semblance of spirit. The first step consists of becoming attentive in the right way to all living things. Every plant emerges not only each spring, it breaks through materialism at all times. The secret of life that bursts from the branches of the trees teaches us to rethink. Just the insight that one no longer comprehends life with the head's thinking creates fresh air for the inner human being. And distant vistas open up. We stand before the lowest level of *that* world which reaches up to the Cherubim and Seraphim. Here, reverence *must* imbue our thinking. A thinking that reckons with the existence of a supersensory world is on the verge of experiencing resurrection. Such a thinking recognizes the supersensory world.

It is not easy to start with thinking. Simultaneously, at least, modern man should commence on a faithful exercise of piety as such. We become free from the deadening treadmill of outer activities if we consciously place ourselves in the spiritual world, feel that we are members of a supersensory world, at least at certain times during the day. This would be the very first beginning of making that innermost activity come alive which we can call 'faith.' We begin to believe, which does not mean that we 'believe in something.' Faith is the power of courage in the soul. Through the extinction of inner activity we have been forced into a defensive attitude regarding life. We are not just afraid of poverty, sickness and death. Fear and apprehension rule our life and cause us constantly to flee our own self. Here, genuine courage is needed. Souls have been weakened completely, because they have no faith. They try to avoid any form of being alone. But without moments of solitude we never find the beginning of the inner path. Only by being alone can I learn to place myself through inner activity into the higher world so that I can say: I lift up my soul to God, I love God. Faith becomes prayer and the soul is saved from its fear, weakness and cowardice. But this must not be egotistic piety. Any egotism causes the human being to be weak. The weakest souls are the crude egotists. Quiet, unselfish people have a thousand times more strength.

The start of a proper Christian prayer is the prayer of devotion, of faith. It grows into the 'prayer in Christ's name.' Like a column of fire, the figure of Christ stands before us when we picture him aglow with the inner activity through which he finally achieved victory over death. The inner activity that we might unfold within can initially be no more than a yearning for this fiery life-will of Christ, a prayer to be allowed to have a share in it. But the more we learn, through the power of faith, to say, 'Not I, but Christ in me,' Christ's prayer flows along with our prayer. His activity imbues our inner activity. With Grace, we receive a share in an element of piety in which not only we as human beings pray and offer up sacrifice. Christ's power of victory and sovereignty of resurrection helps lift up our weakness and allows us to cast off the various constraints of death's spell. We experience the truth of Christ's saying, 'Because I live, ye shall live, also.' This is moreover the mystery of the sacrament celebrated in community with others at the altar. The Resurrected One is active in the souls and bears them up beyond themselves. Joint devotional prayer in Christ's name builds life's kingdom within dying earth-existence.

In the midst of the human spirit's Golgotha and descent into hell the vista opens for the resurrection and ascension of the human spirit; not into a heaven beyond, but into the heaven of spirit-elevation, the actual arising of our true self that is nailed to the cross of matter in us.

The saying from the Old Testament, quoted by Paul a number of times, 'The just shall live by his faith,' indicates that, through the power of faith, a man who brings order to his inner life has the power to seize his life-energy from death and to enhance it. This does not mean that he could extend his outer life. The degree and value of his life-forces increase, the deficit of life is offset. Then, the saying of Christ turns into experience: 'He who believes in me ..., out of his heart shall flow rivers of living water' (John 7:38).

Passion Weeks in the Year's Course

Like nothing else, the bursting forth of spring with the colourful radiant sprouting and growing of buds makes known the magic power of life behind the rhythmic round of the year's seasons. What our senses behold of nature is always merely her earthly physical body. The *life* of nature, her etheric element, already belongs to the supersensory realm. We can become aware of this life, however, in the passage of time. In the sequence of the seasons, in their great swaying rhythm, manifests the sphere of life, the etheric body of our earth, which shows earth to be a mighty, breathing, living being. A true, festive awareness of the seasons in the present and future will become an important path to Christ for the human soul. Through the merciful accommodation of the deity, the first Christ Event had as its stage the tangible, earthly world of facts. Today, the Christ being wishes to manifest in the etheric, in the sphere of life belonging to the earth, a sphere that the Bible indicates in the picture of the cloud. Since his Resurrection and Ascension, Christ is the 'Lord of the heavenly forces on Earth.' And the seasons are the metamorphoses of the heavenly forces working on earth.

Now, it is not simply the natural content and rhythm of the year's seasons as such by means of which we find the sphere of Christ. The colourfully changing thread of nature is entwined into one with the golden thread of the Christian festivals. But we must overcome the unrelated positioning of nature's course and the festival-calendar, which originated above all in the

Protestant era and led to the coining of the term 'ecumenical year.' Altogether, the rightly understood and rightly celebrated festivals form the *Christ-year*, and do so in closest connection with the rhythmic sequence of the annual seasons.

The change of colours on the altars of The Christian Community is an essential support for the soul to learn to feel at home with the pulsating configuration of the year and to encounter in it 'Christ in the Etheric.' In the future, this may well be experienced most strongly, when, as is the case during the four Passion weeks that precede the festival of Easter, the colour of the festival seemingly contrasts sharply with the earth's seasonal garment.

*

As celebrated in the Christian Community, the colour spectrum of the Christian year is comprised of seven segments, each of which is inaugurated by the corresponding festival day, and the mood of the festival continues and closes with its colours and words: Christmas, Epiphany, Easter, Ascension, Whitsun, St John's Tide and Michaelmas. Two festival periods have a preparatory quality inasmuch as they lead to the great annual culmination-festivals of Christmas and Easter: in each case, these are the four weeks of Advent and the Passion weeks. The tenth colour with its fundamental words always emerges between festivals, hence, between Epiphany and Passion, between Whitsun and St John's Tide, between St John's and Michaelmas, and finally between Michaelmas and Advent.

Here, we need to speak in particular of the two festivals that have a preparatory quality. Blue and black signify preparation and preliminary exercise. The blue of Advent helps bring about devotion, inner quiet of world and soul in the unrest of the waning secular year as a preparation towards the bright whiteness of Christmas. The Passion-black, which so radically contradicts the greening and blossoming of awakening spring, allows us to experience the background and substructure of sin and death. All merely natural life possesses this backdrop. It is the grave from which higher life arises, thus preparing us for the red of Easter, the festival of higher life.

Moreover, we become aware of a quiet continuity of growth from Advent-blue to Easter-red. During the time of Epiphany, it appears through the ceremonial, priestly reddish violet, the colour-median between blue and red. The only difference is that the white of Christmas between blue and violet, and the black of Passion between violet and red in each case bring about a festive break, first one of fulfilment, then one of preparation. Due to the fact that, unlike the considerably longer period of Lent in Roman Catholic tradition, we limit the time of Passion that leads to Easter to four weeks, its meaning and quality will manifest in the future more concisely and powerfully. By equating its length of time and the number of Sundays with Advent, its preparatory character becomes quite clear. As a new beginning in the sequence of festivals and colours, the first of the four Passion-Sundays will in time become an important festival, just as the first Sunday of Advent has always been experienced as an important festival despite the preparatory quality of the time that initiated by this Sunday.

*

Giving measure and meaning to the four Passion-weeks is a significant innovation in the history of Christian life. Only the last week before Easter, Holy Week, is observed as the actual period of the Passion in Protestantism where it is a sort of preparation for what follows. But in Protestant tradition, Good Friday is frequently more a culmination of the year than Easter itself. This causes the quality of Passion to extend to the whole year. If nothing else, the predominance of black makes it obvious that, without

clearly intending to do so, Protestants remain in a permanent dis-
position of Good Friday and the Passion.

What differentiates the period of Lent that begins on Ash
Wednesday in the life of the Roman-Catholic Church with the
period of Passion as celebrated in The Christian Community, is
that Lent is not really future-oriented as a preparation. Rather,
it is the result and after-effect of what preceded it. The frolic-
some attitude, expressed in the customs of carnival and
Shrovetide, a period that since the Middle Ages often begins
immediately after Christmas, goes back to humanity's distant
past. When, at the time of the winter solstice, the earth's soul
submerges most deeply into earth's existence, it once
unchained there a whole horde of gnomes, goblins and other
elemental beings who are active in earth-substance. The human
constitution, which until the Middle Ages was completely open
to nature, allowed the effects of these elemental beings to pervade it without inhibition and submitted to their frolicking exu-
berance. In the south, this gave rise to the Roman Saturnalia-
traditions. In the north, it was the origin of the barbarian customs of *Rauhnacht.** The Roman Catholic movement did not
reject these customs, originating as they did in pre-Christian
times, but allowed them to unfold on a Christian basis. Thus,
varying according to different regions, arose the traditions of
carnival.

The impish frolicking had hardly reached its climax when the
medieval Church did a turnabout and put a radical stop to it all.
It decreed that, starting with Ash Wednesday, the stern season
of Lent was to begin. Human beings who up until then had
allowed the effects of the kingdoms of nature to enter them in
boundless manner were now supposed to close themselves off
in a special way against the influences of the earthly forces of

---

* *Rauhnacht* (Rough Night) in German refers to the nights between Christmas and
Epiphany, that is, any one of the twelve Holy Nights

nature throughout the weeks of Lent, above all in what they ingested through food and drink. The pendulum was to swing powerfully over to the other side.

Now, without it having been clearly recognized, the human constitution has long since lost the ancient receptivity for nature's elemental forces. The old carnival-traditions increasingly forfeit their substance and authenticity. This can moreover be observed in the abstract generalization that has taken over the above traditions, inasmuch as people become caught up in the widespread excitement in regions where such customs were formerly quite unknown. It has become clear long since that there can rarely be any more question of genuine inner delight anywhere. And it must probably be realized in quite a new way that, along with the traditions of carnival, fasting too is losing its meaningfulness. Fasting may well retain its purpose as a health measure and acquire even greater significance in the future, but its time as a religious practice is long since over. Human nature has hardened so much that we can do little in regard to affirming or denying the forces of nature, in order, in a healthy sense, to affect our inner life of soul. The efforts of directing and disciplining one's own inner life can attain their goal less and less by external means. These efforts must pursue inner directions. This is the reason why the outwardly preserved conventions of the Lenten season cover up a vacuity that occurred long ago.

*

In the four weeks preceding Easter, a metamorphosis of the once outward fasting must take place which befits the present state of human nature. In so doing, the properly comprehended term 'asceticism' will quite definitely remain valid. The Greek word *askesis* was never a negative concept that implied, for example, that one should not eat or drink certain foods.

Asceticism in the positive sense signifies 'training,' and this originally referred to the training for the Olympic Games in which the best-trained person won the crown of victory.

During the four Passion weeks, the black colour on our altars summons our souls to inner work and discipline. We do not have the right to abandon ourselves to the dawning spring, if, particularly at this time, we do not work on ourselves. The contrast between the radiant colours of nature and the Passion-black at the altar is supposed to point us inward. If we follow this challenge, we find ourselves on the way to the inner sunrise, concealed as it is in the outer spring, which is the secret of the Easter festival.

At the very bottom of all things, even if they are clothed in the splendour and beauty of spring, there slumbers death. In us, too, death is the ruler, in so far as it is the wages of sin. The beginning and principle of pre-Easterly discipline must be for human beings to become aware of their distance from God, their wickedness and weakness. In Protestantism, the theological dictum of the sinfulness of human nature is frequently in use. But in the long run, it is losing its significance for human beings in our days. We deal with a deeply profound truth here that acquires meaning not as a theological dictum but through silent, faithful discipline of the soul. The period of Passion will in the future be quite senseless, if the soul is not filled with the full power of this discipline particularly during this time. For it will be possible from here to bear earnestness and significance to the other segments of the year's course. When man crosses the Easter-threshold from the direction of the four weeks of Passion with the fruit of this faithful discipline, the Easter festival will bestow its light and power more and more abundantly. In the Passion weeks' sacramental words, through which speaks the prostrate, lamenting human 'I,' something of this discipline takes place. Here, an important step leads from the first three Passion weeks to Holy Week. First, the words of the

Act of Consecration cause human beings to sense their inner poverty: empty is the space of the human heart. But then, out of the awareness of the spirit-loss that has led to the inner emptiness, the longing must grow that is kindled like a sacrificial fire in the heart of man: there burns the space of the human heart. Thus, something of the mystery of the 'dying with Christ' is woven into the weeks before Easter, so that, at Easter, the mystery of being 'resurrected with Christ' can touch and fill the soul.

*

The transition from the Passion to the festival of Easter is in a way concealed throughout the whole year in the inner structure of the altar-ritual. Transubstantiation is always preceded by the Offering. Man can thus seek the path to the Resurrection-mystery at any time through the properly conducted Offering. At the beginning of the Offering, those who join in prayer must become aware of their distance from God and their unworthiness: the heart is empty. This is supported by the words through which the one who conducts the Offering denotes himself before God as his 'unworthy creature,' and confesses to his aberrations, his denials of the divine being and his weaknesses. And when the smoke of the incense rises up, this signifies that the fire of the Offering is en- kindled on the altar of the heart: the heart burns. The question might be raised whether it makes sense to add even more difficulties to so much that is difficult in our times by practising self-awareness of one's sinfulness. But this is the same as in the case of genuine compassion. If you suffer along with the suffering of another person or with the objective suffering of humanity, you will come to terms with your own suffering more easily. Nothing gives you more strength for managing the difficulties of life than to train your soul in the faculty of surrender and sacrifice.

When the weeks of Passion turn into a special time for practising sacrifice in the human heart, then purity and depth are
woven into the whole fabric of human life. A religious element
develops that brings all superficiality and illusions of life to an
end.

Holy Week

The annually returning time between Palm Sunday and Easter Sunday is the most wondrous compendium of the Christ-mysteries. A conscious, vigorous comprehension of the qualities of colour and sound inherent in the various days within the rainbow-like octave of this week will in future time be of the greatest help in attaining a larger and more profound picture of the Christ's true being. A path with various stations becomes visible that has universally human greatness and expanse. The holy stations at ancient locations of pilgrimage, in front of which, in strict sequence, the pilgrims carried out their devotional practices, were limited to the actual steps of the Passion, meaning, the scenes that depict the painful Good Friday path by Christ to Golgotha. Due to this, the time before Easter has assumed the one-sided character of the Passion period, that is, the period of suffering. Christ turned into the Man of Suffering whose sight aroused human compassion and self-reproach in the soul, for people saw how the penalties they themselves would have deserved were suffered by another.

It can readily be deciphered from the pictorial calendar of Holy Week that Christ was infinitely more than the tormented Man of Suffering; that in all and everything he is the mightiest warrior and vanquisher. This is the case not only when we move on from Good Friday to Easter Sunday but also when we consider the various stages of the days preceding Good Friday beginning with Palm Sunday. The Easter-victory over death crowns a series of victoriously fought battles. Even behind the seemingly passive endurance of the scourging and crucifixion appears the heroically glowing sovereignty of the victor. The point is that the arena of the battle is increasingly moved from outside to within and in this way Holy Week assumes the character of stillness only after midweek. At the beginning stands the mighty challenge for decisive battle: the entry into Jerusalem on Palm Sunday and the cleansing of the Temple on Monday. A single person challenges the whole world. On Tuesday, the sword of the Word flashes in the replies that Jesus gives to the devious questions of the hate-filled opponents. But thereafter, instead of struggling against humans, battle is waged against invisible opposing forces of the cosmos, finally against death itself. The tomb's stillness on Holy Saturday veils the radiant entry of the victor into the world of the dead, a region that had become the dark world of the shades. At Easter's early dawn, the might of death is itself is bound in chains.

*

As the week of spring's full moon, Holy Week stands out from the whole of the year's course in regard to the cosmic element that holds sway in it. When in reawakened nature the forces of life begin their new creative cycle in joyful abundance of colours and forms, the influence of the seven planetary spheres, linked as it is with the various days of the week, is effective with particular richness of colour and formative force. The primal phenomenon of each day of the week becomes visible more clearly than at other times. One after the other, Moon, Mars, Mercury, Jupiter, Venus, Saturn and Sun have their spring festival day. Defining the various soul-strains, they likewise were effective in the Christ-related contents of that original Holy Week. One after the other, the planetary spirits bowed to the Lord of the cosmos and, serving him on earth, began to transform their being.

Viewed in this way, Holy Week is a significant path from the old to the new sun. On Palm Sunday, the sun-festivals of ancient times extend into the Christ-drama. But the Lord of the Sun now unites with earth through his struggle against the forces of the dark depth. Easter Sunday is the festival of the new sun waxing in earth-existence. The Christ-transformation of the sun is preceded by that of the other planets. They are cosmic processes that accompany the events of the seven days on the level of human destiny in Jerusalem.

*

All that has turned old in the world without retaining its originality and strength, all that has rigidified, as has the moon, and without light of its own, is dismissed on Passion-Monday. In the open, among the people, religious decadence and corruption are censured in the scene of the Temple purification. In the realm of soul, the puzzling 'cursing of the fig tree' represents the renunciation of ancient ecstatic and visionary faculties which, even though they caused the folk on the day before to call out their 'Hosanna,' are on the verge of extinction and no longer dependable.

On Passion-Tuesday, the Mars-forces have to conform to Christ's word-power. Throughout the day, he, whom the enemies are trying to entrap, speaks and replies to his opponents. The parables of the evil vineyard-tenants and the royal wedding are like blows with a sword. In the evening on the Mount of Olives, Christ's word unlocks the apocalypse to the disciples: the future paths of mankind must pass through turbulence and shattering trials, particularly during the age of the second mighty Christ-revelation, which takes place in the etheric realm on the clouds. Perhaps our present age can find particularly factual access to the mysteries of Holy Week inasmuch as it finds that it is reflected in the scenes of Mars-day.

The Wednesday of Holy Week indicates the cross-road at which the mercurial force of the soul's mobility must arrive as humanity advance towards the fiery zone of Christ-proximity: either it degenerates into the restlessness that causes Judas to become the betrayer, or it is transformed into devotional power as Mary Magdalene is able to do.

Maundy Thursday is imbued with the Jupiter-like glistening of a new wisdom. The spirit-nearness of the Sacrament is at the same time a source of light: as narrated by the Gospel of John the words of farewell make evident the wisdom which has completely united with love.

The Christian day of Venus is Good Friday: the manifestation of universal love. That which has to be endured, from the Scourging to the Crucifixion, only demonstrates that love bears all and thereby vanquishes all, even the very power of death.

Finally, Saturn joins in the service of Christ, when the quiet of the tomb and the Sabbath with its leaden gravity draw a veil over the bursting open of hell's portals and the sunrise thus brought about in the realm of the departed.

At last, on earth, the Easter-sun overcomes all the forces of hindrance. In the light-form of the Resurrected One, the seed of a new body and creation makes its appearance.

Golgotha and the Grail

The stern cross of Golgotha questions the newly burgeoning life
of spring. It inscribes the rune of death onto the field of life. It
admonishes us that all natural life, regardless of how bountiful
and joyful it may be, conceals death, the fate of all earthly creatures.

But even as natural death conceals death, so death reveals
true life. Do we not experience it again and again through those
who are dying that death's nearness allows the true nature of
man, hidden behind so many masks and sheaths, to flash forth
momentarily? Did we ever imagine that such majesty can slumber in a wretched, sinful human being? And when the soulless
body lies on the bier and we are moved deeply enough, do we
not gain knowledge through compassion? Is it not given to us
then to seek and find the spirit-form that struggles free of the
body? Certainly, times will come when pain will cause people
to become aware of the soul-spiritual part of the one of whose
presence death had robbed them.

*

Never did death reveal more than in the hour of Golgotha. All
of creation sensed this. Earth shook and trembled to its very
core. The sun turned dark and deepest night reigned for three
hours at noontime. The storm that raged through the elements
was none other than the resistance of the power of darkness. It

had to give up its secret. The Temple's curtain was rent from top
to bottom. Under the covering of death, the dimension of true
life was laid open. The Lord of True Life vanquished the power
of death.

We can begin to imagine the scene: how they nailed him on
the Cross and then lifted the Cross up. Who was watching this?
A throng of strangers who stood around curiously. The disciples
were not present. Torn between fear and hope, crushed by the
sequence of events, they lost their wakefulness. The spell of the
Gethsemane-sleep engulfed their souls. They were not there
because they had no presence of mind. But it does say in the
first three gospels: 'A group of women who had followed Jesus
and his disciples stood at a distance and saw these things' [EB].
The women were more advanced in consciousness, they were
actual witnesses of the drama. How are we supposed to imagine that they watched from a distance? The rock of Golgotha
was located directly outside the gates of the city. Close by the
city wall stretched along and almost directly across was one of
its gates, the 'Garden Gate.' It had this name because to the left
of the bare rock of Golgotha, the Place of the Skull, it led out to
a charming garden area. Atop the wall was a walkway which
widened above the gates. The women stood atop the Garden
Gate and watched the Crucifixion. Bitter pain racked their
souls.

What happened in the minds of the women who participated
with all their heart in the Golgotha event had been experienced
earlier in one of them. It was Mary Magdalene, who had anoint-
ed the feet of the Lord in Bethany. When she did this, her mind
was filled with conceptions similar to those of the others who,
due to the jubilant mood of Palm Sunday, believed that the mission of Jesus among humankind was about to reach its final
breakthrough and rich fulfilment. But deep below the threshold
of her consciousness, she was nonetheless led by a premonition
of the Golgotha tragedy. Jesus openly spoke of it: 'Leave her

alone; she does it even now for my death' [EB]. Mary
Magdalene, wholly a sentient soul, was wiser and more
prophetic in deed than in her thoughts. At the dawn of Easter
morn, out of an equally great, spontaneous emotion, she would
be the privileged one. She would be the first who would at least
have a pre-sentient encounter with the Resurrected One. Even
as she had the profound presentiment of death without har-
bouring the thought of death, she then had the mighty presentiment of the Resurrection without yet knowing what this
meant. During the actual hour of Golgotha, she withdrew, as it
were, for although present, she was totally devastated by
anguish. The inner direction of her being moved from the quiet
hour in Bethany directly across to the morning of Easter.

Another female figure stood out among the group atop the
Garden Gate during the Golgotha-hour. When the actions up
front exceeded all comprehension of a human heart, deep darkness quickly engulfed everything in the uproar of the elements.
Did this blackness mercifully try to veil the horror? It was the
opposite of a curtain; it was a darkening of revelation. It took
away sensory brilliance so that the deeper dimension, which
harbours true light and life, could manifest. One of the women
left the group. She ventured into the darkness to stand below
the Cross. She was the 'Mother of the Lord,' called thus by the
Gospel of John. But she did not venture there in order to behold
something up close that, owing to the darkness, she could not
see from a distance. She went there *because* she saw something.
Something happened there that irresistibly seemed to summon
and attract her.

From the other side, another had stepped into the darkness!
From the circle of the disciples who remained in soul-darkness,
one, namely John, had risen up *because* he had beheld something. Under the Cross, Mary and John met. As yet, the one
on the cross was still alive. He spoke to both of them. Actually,
he did not have to speak, his very being spoke. They beheld

something through him. Must we today not become particularly aware of this secret? More than in words, Christ speaks
through the blood that pours from his wounds. What the two
beheld who were touched and summoned by the tearing of the
curtain, was *the mystery of the blood of Christ.*

How are we to understand this? The Grail-saga, in the images
of which a knowledge of this secret flowed as through isolated
rivulets into later centuries, is based on the conviction that,
every year on Good Friday, the power of the holy Grail — that
is, the power of Christ's blood — is renewed in the sacred chalice inasmuch as the dove of the Holy Spirit descends upon it.
Why does the dove of the Holy Spirit hover over the Grail on
Good Friday? Because it repeats what it did on the first Good
Friday. Then, like a bright stream of light, the dove of the holy
Spirit descended into the midst of the darkness down to where
the blood streamed from the wounds of the Crucified One. In
that hour of death, the Grail Mystery was born.

Through her whole being, Mary was prepared to behold this
miracle. Did the dove of the Holy Spirit not descend upon her
when, directed from above, in the radiance of the sacred spirit-
world, the virginal birth took place? Then she was imbued in
her *very being* by the cosmic virginity of the Holy Spirit. Thirty
years later, in the profound farewell-talk that Jesus had with her
before he went to meet John the Baptist, a first tearing of the
curtain took place.* Her empathy with the humanity-encompassing suffering of young Jesus caused her to gain insight.
Thus, the dove that appeared over the Jordan and illumined the
mighty transformation that occurred in Jesus, hovered at the
same time over the 'Mother of the Lord,' enkindling in her a
new inspired consciousness. At that moment, not only her being
but her *awareness* became imbued and filled with the Holy
Spirit. She experienced the Three Years as a different, trans-

* See also Emil Bock, *The Childhood of Jesus.*

formed person. Whereas, in Mary Magdalene, the sentient soul had true dreams, in her, the consciousness soul entered a new awakening.

Now, she experienced the miracle for a third time. The dove descended to the blood of the Crucified One. And Mary sensed the dove above herself, over her own heart, her own blood. It was this that made her walk into the darkness. And John, who shortly before had been laid in the tomb as Lazarus and had been reawakened as John, belonged particularly among those who could hold a dialogue with the dove of the Holy Spirit.

Just as the scene at Bethany is linked to Easter morning for Mary Magdalene, so, for Mary's soul, the Golgotha hour is connected directly with Whitsun. For in the morning of Whitsun, Mary with her profound understanding was to become the centre of the spirit-illumined circle of disciples. And once again the dove will be above the Grail, except that the Grail will then be the human hearts from which the flames of Whitsun burst forth.

Mary and John remained under the Cross. Two strangers joined them. When even the closest friends failed, witnesses of the miracle quickly drew near from afar. There was a captain from distant northern Europe, who with his lance pierced the side of the Crucified One. And there was Joseph of Arimathea who collected the blood that flowed from the wounds in the sacred cup that served at the Last Supper. These two likewise gained insight in the midst of darkness. The captain said: 'He is truly the Son of God.' And Joseph of Arimathea may have decided at that very moment to go to Pilate and ask that the body be released to him so that he might lay it to rest in his garden next door. When the one who hung on the Cross said to Mary and John: 'Behold, this is your son, behold this is your mother,' a new spiritual blood relationship came into being, because both were permeated in inner vision with the mystery of Christ's blood.

In a special sense, John was henceforth the first among the

brothers of Christ. Words would not even have been required to establish the brotherhood of the Grail as a sacred fact. This brotherhood passed its first test when, in the circle of the disciples, Mary held on her lap the body of the Lord, taken down from the Cross.

*

> Who has guessed the earthly body's lofty meaning?
> And who can say he understands the blood?
> Novalis

Blood is the bearer of life. Together with the blood, life streams out. But the fact that the outpouring of blood signifies loss of life, namely, death, demonstrates that natural life is not yet true, pure life. In our human blood, life and death are mixed together. Our life forces have a mortal nature.

But the life that flowed out on Golgotha with the blood of Christ was a life that could no longer be injured or stunted by death's powers. It was everlasting, incorruptible, eternal life. This life possessed the radiantly golden, etheric light-form that broke through the spell of the noon-hour's darkness. In it, for the first time, the Grail shone forth brightly.

Our blood is not only affected by the oxygen in the air or by what we eat and drink. The mark of transformation we inscribe by way of the warmth element into our blood through what happens in us soul-spiritually due to our thinking, feeling and will is much more important.

Most of all, we provide our blood with more death than life because of our dead thinking, in fact, with almost nothing but death. Not only is outer civilization filled with elements of death these days, but above all, human blood.

Christ's blood was entirely spiritualized from within and therefore purely the bearer of life. Indeed, it was *life itself*. If, through the properly practised triad of faith, hope and love, we reach the point of being able to say with inner justification: 'Christ in me,' we will experience how the blood and life of Christ begins to flow within our own blood. We will sense how the invisible temple-dome of the Grail-community begins to arch over us.

Behold, this is Man!

The Easter jubilation to which people in former times could blissfully surrender must first be re-learned by human beings nowadays. Neither can the great allegory of re-arising spring-nature still speak clearly and powerfully to us, nor can we rejoice over an event that occurred two thousand years ago, regardless of how great a miracle it was. At Easter, the Act of the Consecration of Man speaks of the delightful rejoicing that fills the realm of the earthly atmosphere. But the natural awakening of spring as such is not yet the exulting hymn of praise that nature will one day strike up because Christ was resurrected. The new life of spring existed in nature even prior to the Christ-event, but it was initially merely an anticipated prophecy. Has it now turned into the celebration of a fulfilment that has come to pass?

Nature cannot rejoice over a historic fact. It awaits a force that is effective in the direct present. As yet, the mystery of Easter does not exert its influence in spring's nature. Nature awaits man. The words of rejoicing and illumining the breath of earth are followed in the Act of the Consecration of Man by the sentence that expresses the condition for this: before this happens, Christ must have moved into man's jubilant pulse of life. And only the Easter-jubilation of the human being whom the Resurrected One indwells, turns nature's jubilation, which in itself is merely a prophetic hope, into actual fulfilment.

Man learns Easterly rejoicing in the school of Pauline

Christendom. The saying, 'I live, yet not I, but Christ lives in me,' is the key to the Easter mystery. The thought of Christ's Resurrection must not merely exist in our souls, but he himself, and in such a way that he is constantly resurrected in us. Creation will then take note of this so that through man's jubilation the hymn of rejoicing will be evoked in creation, even if outwardly human beings continue to ruin nature and cause it to become ugly. In man begins the resurrection of the world.

*

'Behold, this is man!' Regardless of whether these words are audible to human ears or not, they resound from the stations of the Gospel leading to the Easter festival. Pilate uttered them first when he displayed the one to the bawling crowd, who was beaten bloody, wore the crown of thorns and the scorn-provoking purple mantle. Through him, who was more royal than a king, we are to realize that man is a distorted king.

Again, the saying resounded from the three crosses that stood on Golgotha in the darkness at noon. Indeed, before one of the crosses of an evil-doer, we can become aware how a voice in us says: 'This is you!' Our culpability oppresses us and we recognize ourselves in the evil-doers on the crosses. But before the cross in the middle, the words, 'Behold, this is man!' and addressed to us: 'This too is you!' are even more valid. How can this be? The cross of guilt bears the most innocent one in the world. How dare I relate this to myself? Christian Morgenstern taught us how:

> I have seen man's profoundest form.
> I understand the world to the very core.
> I know that love, love is its deepest purpose,
> And I am here, for ever more to love.
> I spread my arms out like he did,
> Like he, I would embrace the whole wide world.

Then the stories of Easter light up. Even when viewing the figure of the Resurrected One, we should aspire to hear the words and relate them to us: 'This is Man!' It is not a miracle that confronts us, for instance the oddity that a man rises out of the grave the same way he was laid in it. No, we behold the destiny is of each and every human being in perfection. Here, just this once, the goal has been reached, in the face of which we only too easily back away in discouragement: *the Spirit Man.* This is the Resurrected One.

How do we find the way to actualize this human condition in us that confronts us here in its Easter-configuration? We human beings sense our impotence. How ineffective we are in regard to our physical surroundings! We can only destroy them. The fact that we have learned to destroy it so grandiosely today gives us the illusion of power. But it is only a semblance of man's power over matter; for we basically do not even know what we are doing when we produce super-dimensional explosions. We cannot create anything that lives or is endowed with a soul. Sickness and death rule over us. We can doctor around a little. But in the end are delivered up to the tyranny of death. Why are we so powerless? Because man's spiritual part, which does hover over us, does not intervene. As earthly human beings, we initially are noting but a fragment, an empty vessel. As yet, we do not even inhabit our bodily sheaths at all with our innermost being. How, therefore, could the spirit that does not dwell within the sheaths affect these sheaths and, through them, the physical surroundings?

We dwell within a spirit-devoid habitation on earth. Our human existence is a desecrated temple. The dogma of the year 869, which states that man consists merely of body and soul, does in fact describe man as he *still* is. But at the same time it also expresses this dogma's untruth and lack of faith. Man not only consists of body and soul but moreover of that being of genius which is to live in these sheaths and, seedlike, does live in them even now. To the extent that it enters into them, this actual Spirit-I of man can transform the human sheath-nature. The 'I' not only can order and harmonize the soul, it moreover can make it transparent. It establishes peace inwardly and the ability to love outwardly. The spiritualized soul begins brilliantly to radiate. When the spirit-essence of man takes hold of the sheaths, it finally penetrates not only the soul but beyond that even our body and our blood — blood as bearer of our life.

Soul, life and body can be irradiated and transformed from within. But as yet, the spell of estrangement from God, sin, burdens the human being. The meaning of the Christ-event, from the Incarnation in a human being all the way to the Resurrection, is contained in the fact that the most sublime ego, the 'I' of humanity, has moved into the desecrated temple, into the empty and impure vessel of man's being. The body of a man became the stage of a mighty drama of transformation. Here, for the benefit of all men, the human form was inwardly completely filled and taken hold of by the spirit. A sacred fire blazed during the three years of Christ's life. It caused the earthly sheaths, soul, life and body to glow and melt through and through. The blood that finally flowed from the wounds of the Crucified One was spiritualized life; it was Life Spirit, eternal life. And the body that was laid in Joseph of Arimathea's tomb was in the end merely an outer indication of a spiritual body, of a bodily sheath wholly transformed by the spirit's fire, of Spirit-Man himself. What occurred in the drama of the life of Christ, in the Incarnation, the Death on Golgotha and the Resurrection, was the fulfilment of the Being of Man for the first time in all its greatness. The one who emerged from the grave was the first perfect human being. In the man, Jesus of Nazareth, the fundamental sentence coined later by Paul, 'Not I, but Christ in me,' was realized in unique majesty. It was the first, but at the same time the most perfect indwelling of Christ in human nature.

Henceforth, every human being can turn into the dwelling of Christ. It is not an alien 'I' that moves into a human being and brings about transformation. We are then more than ever our own selves, because the Christ-I is the higher ego of all human beings. The indwelling of Christ awakens the slumbering seeds of Spirit-Man in the human soul. The Christ-I helps our own true 'I' to enter and be active, helps it to become effective in the spiritualization of our whole nature, so that we experience the mystery of resurrection. Only a Christian begins to be a complete human being. Without the indwelling of Christ, man is a fragment for all time. Our spirit indwells us only through Christ.

In no way can genuine indwelling be linked to a passive attitude. It signifies innermost, fire-related activity. Paul does not say that we die and re-arise *through* Christ. We are to go *with* him through death and resurrection. This refers to the covenant that Christ in us makes with our own true self. He turns our spirit into the fiery flame that attains Easter's victory over death. Through the supportive power of the Resurrected One, we can exert a transforming influence from within on our sheaths, even if it is only in allusive ways and presentiments. And particularly at Easter time, we may feel at home in the sphere of transformation, which is the world of spirit-corporeality.

*

Easter's Act of the Consecration of Man speaks three times of jubilation. Nature can be jubilant when, through the Easterly Christ-influence, the innermost pulsation of life begins to be jubilant in man. Finally, there resounds the hymn of praise concerning the 'rejoicing, healing power' that proceeds from the pulse-beat of the Christ-enwarmed heart. A physician is sensed who heals the world through the joy of Easter's exultation. This is the man of Easter in us. Maybe he is as yet delicate and in a germinating state. But the butterfly moves in the cocoon. One day it will push through its housing and unfold its wings. And when the butterfly emerges, the true jubilation of Easter is regained for soul-impoverished humanity.

Easter and the Cosmos

At Easter, we can meet one another with a radiant greeting of joy, as do the Christians of the Eastern Church since early Christian times. After all, Easter is the birthday of a new cosmos, the everlasting birth-moment of a new earth and a new heaven. The proper joy of Easter has cosmic dimensions. Creation and the realm of the elements join in man's celebration at Easter-time. The environs of earth's atmosphere rejoice in delight.

From the depths of the pushed open earthly tomb, the Resurrected One arises and nature blossoms in new light. Mary Magdalene is the first witness of the new life all around. In the garden, she beholds the Gardener. Henceforth, year after year, the blossoms of the magic of Good Friday and Easter mingle with natural spring. Forty days later, his disciples behold how the Resurrected One fully and wholly becomes Lord of the Elements.

A reversal of the Fall occurred on Good Friday and Easter. Since time immemorial, everything was involved in a downward movement. Man fell and forced creation ever more deeply into earth's substance. Now, succeeding the tragic Fall, the upward movement begins, and it is not coincidental that burgeoning spring is the season for the Easter-process. Year after year, we experience an ever growing sphere: the earth's soul rises from the earth's depths and enters upon her journey to heaven, her ascension, and the miracle of resurrection, the sphere of the Resurrected One, grows along with it, beginning with Easter morn. We can even sense ascension's upward drive starting early on at the Easter festival. Christ has moved into the rhythm of earth-life. It was not a magic act of the gods that created the new cosmos, so that it would have been present once and for all from then on. If that were the case, it would be much simpler to celebrate Easter. We would merely have to observe a great festival of gratitude for the cosmic miracle that was brought about by the gods without the collaboration by humanity. Moreover, it would not be essential to pass actively through the inner steps of the stations of Passion Week prior to Easter in order to earn the right to celebrate this festival. Yet it is one of the most profound Christian truths that the events which preceded Easter morn are supposed to make it possible for our souls to find a creative connection to the ongoing Easter process. We must learn to suffer and die with Christ. Year after year, throughout our whole life, we must make progress in this. After all, the prerequisite for the ascension of the new cosmos that was born at Easter time is that human beings play their part in it. It depends on us whether the seed of Easter comes forth.

*

In four sentences, we can try to express the Easter mystery which, on the whole, is still obscured today:

'The deity did not create the world from outside but from within.' This refers to the original creation of the world.

'The world fell ill and deteriorated not from outside but from within.' This was the Fall.

'The healing of the world does not take place from outside but from within.' This is the meaning of the Mystery of Golgotha.

'The new creation of the world does not occur from outside but from within.' This is what we are involved in through the annual observance of the Easter festival. We are relied upon as the coworkers of God regarding the future of the world.

The first world-creation did not simply take place from outside. Out of its innermost being, the deity let stream the will of love. This then condensed to cosmic warmth. The fire of God's love is the world's primal condition. And when creation progressed and condensed further, the other elements were added. To warmth, the elements of air and water were added. Finally, the solid earth crystallized from all this. This is what the creation-story of the Old Testament refers to when it describes how the spirit of Gold brooded over the primal waters. Since the ancient languages use the same word for spirit and air, moreover, since the pictorial term, 'to brood,' points to the emanation of warmth, the reference is actually to warmth, air, water and earth. On the celestial ladder of the elements, creation descended to itself out of the heart of God. In man, the world's creation found its completion for the time being. In him, a small world came into being, a microcosm that reflects the macrocosm, the great world. Man likewise had to built up his corporeality out of the four elements. We not only have a physical body. In the life forces of our organism, we are dependent on the watery element; in our soul, on the breath, the wafting of the divine wind in the world; in the element of warmth, we may dwell as spirit-beings. When man still corresponded wholly to God's creative intentions, when he was only on the verge of incarnating in earth's solidifying physicality, in him too, the spiritual hovered over the primal waters.

But then the whole world became distorted. By what? The Fall was not caused from outside but from within, outward. A tempter-power approached and lured man, who still hovered as a spiritual being over the flowing segment of his earthly nature, to descend faster and earlier than had been intended. When the spirit of man no longer remained hovering over the watery element but descended; when the warmth-element immersed into the fluid, watery element, blood originated which was susceptible to the incitements of the tempter. In the blood, man's being then rigidified. Life, tied as it is to the watery element, became darkened and falsified. Death entered the human being. Sin penetrated man's blood, and the wages of sin were death. Moreover, since all of nature was still at the point of developing, man dragged the kingdoms of creation along in his fall. Thus originated what we today call matter, earthly substance with its gravity. Wholly from within, the world became sick.

Since the sickness of the world originated in us, healing, likewise must begin in us. And because sickness originated in our blood, healing likewise must start there. This is the mystery of our blood, retained still by God, that here, the warmth-element of our being in which we dwell is spiritually united with the fluid element that bears our life forces. We cannot directly influence our corporeality with our inner being. Our spirit cannot simply transform matter. But everything that takes place inwardly in us affects the warmth. Beginning with turning red or pale, what goes on in our soul is mirrored by the blood. Through our inner being, we have an effect on our body, though initially only on its warmth-segment. But from there, the effect of our inner being continues on to the breath, the airy element; furthermore to the watery or life element and finally the solid element of our physical body. If man's ego were not weakened by the Fall and estranged from itself, based on his own forces, man could bring about an upward evolution where the evolutionary trend had gone downward. Beginning with the blood, he could overcome the consequences of the Fall. But here, the tragic limitation of human nature becomes quickly evident. Increasingly, man became subject to death's tyranny. Then Christ became Man. In him, who for three years walked on earth in human form, dwelt an ego that was strong enough first to wrest the blood away from the opposing powers and then to spiritualize it through and through. This was the miracle of

Good Friday when the blood flowed from the wounds of the Crucified One and turned into the contents of the Grail. What had begun in Christ's blood as the great, new miracle of creation, continued. On the third day, even the earthly body had been wrested from death, having turned wholly into spirit-form. This signified the healing of the world. Good Friday stands for the completely spirit-infused blood, Easter stands for the utterly spirit-pervaded body. They were the firstborn components of the new heaven and new earth.

*

Now we have to find the connection to what Christ has accomplished for us. We must seek for him at the beginning, not at the end. We cannot immediately count on a share of Easter without having acquired the share of Good Friday. And we attain a share in the new world only from out of our innermost being, and this is by allowing Christ's blood to stream in our blood. As a confession of mere words the sentence, 'Not I, but Christ in me,' signifies nothing. We must make it real in us in such a way that we could also say: not my blood, but the blood of Christ in my blood. That is *faith*. But faith means receiving the blood of Christ into one's own blood, opening one's heart, so that a higher element can pulsate in the veins. When Christ dwells within us, a power is in us that conquers death, meaning, in every single drop of blood. The saying, 'If one is in Christ, one is a new creature,' is a true Easter-pronouncement. If a person can rightfully say, 'Christ in me,' then the new creation begins in him or her, the new cosmos is born in such a one. At Easter time, words that can become an inner guideline for us resound from our altars. They refer to the warmth that transforms the heart's beat into a 'rejoicing, healing power.' Yes, it must be warmth, but not the warmth that can be diminished by our heart's coldness. It has to be the creative warmth of a new

primal beginning, the love of Christ. We may rejoice, because
Christ's pulse-beat pulsates along with our heart, because in
our veins his blood streams along with ours.

If the blood's warmth-transformation is attained in the sign
of Good Friday, then, at Easter, the other word of 'rejoicing' is
rightfully pronounced, namely, that Christ has moved into
man's jubilant life-pulse. At the same time, the word from
which we proceeded turns fully into truth, the one of rejoicing
in delight, in which the 'airy regions of the earth' participate. If
the rejoicing does not begin in man, creation likewise cannot
celebrate Easter.

Paul speaks of creation's groaning in travail. At Easter, we
must and indeed may speak of the rejoicing of all creatures. Still,
not as something that comes by itself. For Paul says in the same
sentence that creation waits with eager longing for the revealing
of the sons of God, and this means, nature awaits the human
being. It is quite correct to coin these words in the following
way: the kingdoms of creation wait with longing for the sons of
God finally to begin to shine forth among human beings. When
the green of Easter rays forth from the red of man's warm blood,
then the green of spring with all its blossoming around us at last
receives its meaning. Not until we have paid the innermost
sacred tribute to nature by offering up to her the radiance of the
Christ-being, do we have the right to be gladdened by spring.
The essential word of Good Friday is: 'Christ in us.' By comparison, the essential Easter word is: 'We in Christ.' For then, he
who is greater than we, is in us. He is in us and at the same time
around us, because he radiates out of us.

Christ is present in our world, in our presence. But, spoken
humanly, he is homeless among human being. He ceases to be
homeless where human beings make real the words, 'Christ in
me,' inasmuch as they offer him their hearts as his abode. At the
same time, homeless man finds his home in Christ, because he
receives the One into himself who, like a sphere, grows and rays

forth out of the very centre of his own being. Easter is a whole sphere, in which we can attain a home and civic rights. When we learn during the time of Easter to say, 'We in Christ,' then all around us, through the love-emanation of our heart, a new creation comes about. And even if this can only be alive in the most humble beginning stages, it is nevertheless fitting to call out to one another in grateful joy over the birth of the new cosmos: 'Christ has arisen!' and each replies: 'Yes, he has truly arisen!'

Christ, Lord of the Elements

Forty days after Easter, a world-transforming event illuminates the souls of the disciples. They had been together in a house for forty days. The room on Mount Zion in Jerusalem had been their refuge. It made it possible for them to be in a condition of inwardness, of collecting their thoughts. Thus they could have at their table the guest whose presence was for them a mighty riddle and at the same time a reason for such great exultation, the constant source of Providential recognition. Acts does relate that the Resurrected One was in their midst for forty days and taught them about the mysteries of the kingdom of God. Then destiny brought it about at one time that they were privileged to experience the presence of this guest anew outside in nature on the summit of the Mount of Olive, not at the table in the Cenacle but at the flower-decorated table of nature's spring. The way the figure of the Resurrected One manifested to them was strangely different and quite new. It was in the process of growing and rose before their souls in increasing prominence of light. The Resurrected One in the sphere of the elements — something unheard-of! The world all around, air and atmosphere filled with plant-growth and the scent of blossoms, the pressing of new life, it all harmonized strangely with the light and warmth that emanated from his figure. What sort of disconcerting new secret was this: Christ, the Lord of the elements?

But barely had the disciples perceived him with their visionary souls when it was this very realm of the elements, the atmosphere of earth's air, that took him away before their eyes. Only now, he had truly disappeared from them. And the gift of Providence, which had taken place in the inner composed space of the Cenacle for forty days, was not repeated. He had passed over into a different state of existence. Only for one moment, when he entered the great transformation, it had been possible for the disciples to experience him. Deep, grave sadness was the substance of the ten days that followed until, at the hour of sunrise on Whitsun morning, a first groping answer touched their questioning souls. Once again, they were in the room of the forty days. And all of a sudden, a powerful conviction grew in their minds which told them: he is not far from us; that moment on Ascension Day did not remove him from us — no, he is even closer to us now than he was before. They felt him within themselves; the fiery flame of Christ's indwelling arose in their hearts from a glimmering spark. They experienced how they themselves were carried along into the process of growth, a process that, ten days earlier, had taken him away from their sight. This not only gave them consolation but motivation and strength. It led them out into the world and turned them into apostles.

Still, we must ask whether the disciples did receive a full answer through the Whitsun event to the question which the Providential and then unrelentingly extinguishing moment of Ascension had aroused in them. The riddle remained open. When would their experience on the Mount of Olives continue: the Resurrected One, received like a king in his glory by creation in the realm of the elements?

*

Around Ascension, we are surrounded by the profusion of flowers in springtime. Everything blossoms more lavishly and splendidly than at other times. The secret of the blossom belongs together most intimately with the secret of Ascension. For what causes plants and trees to bloom? How does this miracle come about, in the face of which we are not astounded over and over again simply because we have long since become much too accustomed to it? The spring-sun entices the earth's soul to rise up, and so she soars up from the earth's depths to which she had withdrawn during winter. Then, earth is covered all around with the green abundance of new life. But at this point it is still earth that is revealed when the meadows sprout and the green foliage bursts from the branches. Earth demonstrates that she has decided to let her soul ascend. And then, all at once, appear white, red and all the colourful shades of the flowers. This is no longer earth alone. She could not bring this forth, if the soaring and ascending of her soul would not have reached up to where an answer from heaven, filled with being, comes to meet her. The greening is still from earth, the blossoms are already from heaven. The blossoming all around us indicates the earth's very soul is in a state of ascension, of a rising up which has already led to a touching with heaven. In bridal surrender, earth has been able to wed heaven.

In the flowering, an ascension of the earth's soul reaches its goal. Heaven, to which she aspires, is not a pale beyond. It is the supersensory sphere that supports and penetrates all of our earth's existence, yet it is only near where upward-surging forces prevail that break the spell of this material world. Every spring, earth produces such upward-rising forces. Does the whole of nature not indicate this in a thousand wondrous allegories? A tree is really nothing but a question as long as it is leafless. But when it is adorned with green foliage, does it not replicate earth with its crown, as if its trunk were only the means through which earth offers up a likeness of herself to heaven? Earth makes manifest her will to surge upward, to ascend. And when the same crowns, first on the cherry trees, and then on pear and apple trees, are covered over with blossoms, it is as if heaven, to which earth rises up a thousand-fold, would say: you, earth, you can be a heaven. And all at once, the replicas of earth in the crowns of trees turn into a far-spread, gladdening field of replicas of heaven on earth. And when the blossoms begin only too soon to fall to the ground, is our fearful shiver, evoked as it is by the quick transience, justified? For it was only just a moment that allowed us to perceive heaven's radiance. A faint shadow of the loss, which the disciples suffered so quickly after the light of Ascension had shone forth, has come over us. And when the blossoming splendour has disappeared ten days after Ascension, does the subsequent festival bring the comforting solution that was offered so long ago by Whitsun morning? Even as the briefly blossoming secret of Ascension matured to the flames of Pentecost in the hearts of the disciples, the colourful blossoming in nature is followed by the Pentecostal flame-like ripening of the pistils. Millions of invisible Whitsun-flames, which arouse in us a presentiment of future gifts from heaven, replace the visible lustre of colours. Just as the blossoms were not from the earth but from heaven, so too, afterwards, the fruits on the trees are gifts from heaven to the earth, after-effects, issues of the celestial journey undertaken by the earth's soul. In the same way, even if the apostles could not fully comprehend this as yet, Whitsun was a result of the mighty transformation they had become cognisant of in the being of Christ on the Mount of Olives. The fruiting began which proceeded from the flowering. Surrounded by the flame of ripening, human souls themselves were the pistils.

*

Some day, through a properly understood celebration of Ascension, the concept of Ascension will have become a fundamental principle of faith. Then, Christian life will unfold quite a different mood than in the past. There is probably not a better, more beautiful expression for the practical application of the instruction nature offers us at Ascension-time than the verse by Angelus Silesius:

Blossom forth, frozen Christian, May is outside your door.
You are forever dead, if you don't blossom now and here.

Being a Christian is supposed to become a condition in humanity that can be described as one of blossoming. But does a person today blossom forth because they are Christian? How can we fulfil the Ascension-challenge by Angelus Silesius? What is it that causes the frozen Christian to blossom forth?

Here, new access to the mystery of *prayer* opens up to us. True prayer is a blossoming of the soul. According to the attitudes of Christian development up to now, this may seem paradoxical. We are used to the idea that prayer means entering into the ultimate solemnity of self-reproach. It is true that the cultivation of prayer belongs among the most serious subjects in life. Still, if done rightly, the soul blossoms forth through it. And in the course of the year, the festival of Ascension could well be the mighty hour of instruction in prayer. Then prayer is not self-constriction, praying turns into adoration, into the inner uplifting of the soul, a liberation from earth's weight. A striving to heaven is linked with this, even as something like this is connected outside in nature with the blossoming of the plant-kingdom. Any egotism in prayer shrinks the soul and causes man to sour. But prayer that turns into adoration, because one does not merely pray because of personal wishes and concerns but thanks God and praises Him, allows the soul to grow beyond herself. To the realm that lifts up the earth's soul, as is shown us by nature's flowering, is added as a correspondence the realm that lifts up the human soul.

In the allegory of Ascension, does nature not turn into a temple-sphere in which a sacred act is being celebrated? But we must not cling to the abstract conceptions according to which heaven is a distant hereafter, separated from the worldly realm by an unbridgeable chasm.

We are not separated by so and so many light years from heaven. Only one step separates us from it which we surmount by the uplifting of our soul. *Without* this uplifting, we are stuck fast in the world here. *With* it we touch heaven just as does earthly nature when the trees blossom. Is it not a sacramental mystery that is connected with the blossoming outside? When the chalices of the blossoms are lifted up to heaven by the millions so that heaven can fill them with its content, are we not familiar with this from our experience before the altar, where we also find ourselves in a school of prayer? At the altar, the chalice is lifted up, a visible indication is carried out for the soul's inner ascension-movement. And when the scent of flowers and blossoms streams out, is it not as if incense were rising up at the altar of nature? In front of the altar of the Sacrament, incense is a way of making visible the worship-filled devotion that strives up to heaven. A wondrous analogy exists between the temple of spring and the temple of the altar, between nature's gesture of ascent when she is in bloom and the soul when we pray.

The motif of ascension reveals a secret accord between nature and religion. There are enough areas in life where discrepancies divide piety from commonplace events, where nature and spirit cannot harmonize; but at Ascension they find one another and both express the same idea. From the allegory of spring-nature's ascending magic, we then can learn something for the quieter arising of our soul. It is part of the essential content of ritual and the sacrament, it is the meaning of worship in front of the altar that human beings work here on finding heaven on earth. This distinguishes ritualistic devotion from all merely instructive moralistic preaching that here a heaven arches over human beings into which they can immerse themselves.

Like the blossoms that come into being outside because the plant-kingdom can immerse itself into heaven here on earth, so we may grow into the mystery of blossoming prayer because the heaven of divine presence surrounds us.

In fact, the concept of ascension illuminates the very essence of religion in general. For once, attention has to be drawn to this, because so much 'non-ascending' religion has come about in the world. The Latin re-ligio means 'reunion.' How else are we to unite once again with heaven whence we originated except by such praying and worship in which dwells the secret of ascension? One day, when the Festival of Ascension has attained its full meaning and radiating power, true religion will once again exist on earth.

With the thought of ascension, we pass through the Act of the Consecration of Man. Following the words of the Gospel, when the congregation conducts the Offering, in which the ascension-images of the up-lifted chalice and the rising incense unfold, we stand throughout the whole year within a living ascension-process. We learn to offer up sacrifice, meaning, to grow, rise up and leave the confines of self with our soul. The Offering is followed by Transubstantiation, just as Whitsun follows Ascension, namely, when in the pistils the ripening process fits heaven's gifts into earth-existence. Prayer is heard: heaven answers it through its earth-transforming blessing. In the advance from Offering to Transubstantiation, an eternal spring, a constant flowering and bearing of fruits could be entwined into the year's course. If, for example, in the Act of the Consecration of Man, the sentence, that the grace of the Spirit-God may stream earthward, even as this Offering strives heaven-ward, repeatedly returns, an ascension-prayer in the most literal sense weaves in this throughout the whole year. We are asking for the Whitsun-miracle of a higher fruiting, the Spirit's grace-filled power. And the prayer itself is a flowering upward to heaven by the devout soul. Then, heaven's grace may well lead eventually to the point where human beings who take Christianity seriously have more joyous countenances, that in the midst of all exhausted withering, they are men and women whose souls flower.

*

What really happened forty days after Easter? What was it that shone forth to the disciples on the Mount of Olives like a mighty cosmic presentiment and yet, at the same time, like an unsolved question? The Resurrected One entered a new stage of his own evolution. The progressive transformation of the Christ-being's form can be illuminated by the words in the Act of the Consecration of Man. When, in the third part, prior to arriving fully at the elements of bread and wine, the mystery of transubstantiation touches the forces of the human soul, reference is made to the transformed thinking in which the painful death of Christ, his resurrection and revelation are henceforth alive. Here, the word 'revelation' designates the condition into which Christ entered after passing through death and resurrection. In this sense, that event which the disciples experienced forty days after Easter is the beginning of the revelation. How are we to understand this? The heaven into which the Resurrected One arose at that point is the sphere out of which his revelation can stream to us. Words such as 'revelation' can and must be taken today once more in their full weight. If considered rightly, they are so unheard-of that we ought not to hear or utter them without their taking our breath away. We have to allow them to shake us awake.

So, what is 'revelation'? Let us call to mind the scene on the Mount of Olives just as Acts describes it (1:9): '... And when he had said this, as they were looking on, he was lifted up' — he grew, his form became larger, the disciples had to look up, as it were, in order to be able to follow him — 'and a cloud took him

out of their sight.' This does not indicate a cloud that suddenly
appeared close to the ground and caused a figure who earlier
had stood there to become invisible. The cloud is the whole
atmosphere, the whole sphere of forces where, under the influence of warmth, the watery element rises up so as to condense
as clouds and fall again as rain or dew. The realm of the elements took him away. How can this be? Not that he was no
longer there, but he advanced to a different sphere. The disciples could still barely behold him when he entered this sphere;
but when he fully occupied it he had become so powerful that
their eyes could no longer follow him. They no longer beheld
him because their faculty of vision no longer sufficed to see him.
How wondrous it is to behold the sun when it rises in the morning. But when it rises higher, it gradually acquires so much light
that we no longer can look at it. Then we literally no longer see
the sun due to so much light. And if we nevertheless look into
it, the light blinds us. This is what happened to the disciples
when they followed him with their eyes. Ascension is not a dis-
appearance into an unreachable realm beyond. The heaven that
took him in is the sphere of the supersensible in our sense
world.

'Two men stood by them in white robes.' Earlier, the two figures had appeared to the women by the tomb. They said: 'Men
of Galilee, why do you stand looking into heaven? This Jesus,
who was taken up from you into heaven, will come in the same
way as you saw him go into heaven.' What does this mean? He
has not left and can therefore not really return. He will come
back when, as it were, men's inner faculties, the soul's ability to
see, have expanded and followed him. Now, an inner growth
has to take place in humankind as well. Men's consciousness
must expand. For what does it mean that he will come in the
same way as he disappeared? A curve links Ascension with the
'Second Coming' The cloud had taken him in. And it says in the
Gospels: 'He will come on the clouds of heaven.' In the light of

the hour of Ascension, this word of the Gospel means that we may seek Christ in the realm of the elements where, in the earthly realm, air, water and warmth combine in order to bring about growth, advance and descent, the remarkable succession of forces. Christ disappeared from the visible realm because human souls were unable to follow him. But through the power of Christ the inner force in us can and must grow until we perceive him again or at least can sense his proximity once again.

*

According to the words of the Act of the Consecration of Man, the 'cloud' is the sphere of 'revelation.' Today, we can only say humbly that it *will* be the sphere of revelation. But we can know: even though we are still blind, whence he disappeared he will reveal himself to us. We learn to direct the ascension-impulse to this very sphere. From here, it becomes evident what an unheard-of saying is contained at the beginning of the Act of the Consecration of Man. The first sentence that is spoken at the altar asks for worthiness to conduct the sacred act 'out of the revelation of Christ.' We step under the sphere into which the Resurrected One expanded. The power of the uplifting impulse of our prayer is to bear us to this sphere. The totality of the Act of the Consecration of Man is to be nothing else than for us to rise up to where he can reveal himself to us. Thus, in order to express the inner activity required to receive the cup, the power of confession mentioned that will unite us with what is revealed through Christ.

Worshipping must simultaneously be a confession. Why? Because it is not enough if only feeling rises up. When the conscious, thinking human is involved, worship becomes testimony. To testify to Christ is an advanced form of praying to Christ, for we as cognizing human beings are then within the prayer. Prayer actually does not mean that I receive something but that

I give something, namely that I give myself up, surrender. Worship, confessing, is the meaning of prayer. But when, in confessing, I grow into revelation, testimony turns into cognition. It is then no longer a mere physical, superficial cognizing: the Providence of revelation inclines to our consciousness. When we truly acquire the right of domicile in the ascension-sphere of the Sacrament, where the human soul blossoms in the light of God's Providence through prayer, we will become increasingly conscious Christians. In the inner realm, we will know better and better what we are to become. Certainty will enter our souls. How will this come about?

To those who gather in the right way before the altar with others and increasingly cultivate the art of prayer, ideas will arise in their minds that differ from earlier ones, without their always being aware of it immediately. They hit on better thoughts and know what decisions they should make and in what directions they should go. One can be a most industrious person and have much success or failure — but in time nothing truly fruitful comes to mind any more. At most, one has thoughts that are clever, but they no longer suffice for actual human existence. But a praying, confessing person, who knows and practices something of the uprising forces of the ascension-mystery, will have light-filled thoughts. The world to which that person aspires will begin to manifest to him or her. It is as if that world would condense into a cloud and out of it a golden shower were to fall on this person. This need not instantly occur in the form of significant supersensory experiences or brilliant discoveries, but one is blessed as a self-aware human being. Not only feeling, but human consciousness likewise can be blessed. And we begin to understand why of all festivals it is Pentecost that follows after Ascension. Why have people never taken it fully seriously that the first new manifestation of the Resurrected One consisted of the fact that the disciples were inspired, that they received the Holy Spirit? The concept of

Pentecost was at most given a central position among sectarian groups who believed that the Holy Spirit signified ecstatic peculiarities. The essence of the Holy Spirit is revelation, inspiration. Of course, impatience must not cause us to forfeit coming under the cloud of Ascension and the Second Coming and thus finding the way to the festival of Pentecost.

The secret that an ever-present Whitsun follows an ever-present Ascension must train us to have the patience of true prayer and devotion. But certainty can and shall be our lot even with the very first steps on this way by which we draw nearer the world of revelation, for we are even then substantially touched by that world. The heaven in which we may seek the Resurrected One is not in a distant world beyond. Standing in our world on this side within the tasks we must fulfil here, we can be near to the one who has become 'the Lord of the heavenly forces on earth.' In us and through us, the first fruits of 'Christ's revelation' can ripen on earth. At the festival of Ascension, the Act of the Consecration of Man speaks of the Christ-permeated world on this side by turning to Christ who dwells in the earthly world, glorifying Earth-existence with heavenly existence. The light of Christ's revelation, the Glory of God, does not merely radiate high above us. Through the mystery of Transubstantiation, it likewise shines out of the realm of earth-elements as a growing light of transfiguration. Even as spring's heaven evokes a reflection of heavenly radiance in blossoming earth-nature, so the sphere of Christ's revelation creates a light-mirror everywhere, where in man and in creation the radiance of transfiguration begins.

The Festival of Ascension

The festival of Ascension contains the seed of a future cosmic Christianity, inasmuch as it instructs us about the true relationship between heaven and earth. It shows us how, through the Mystery of Golgotha, the chasm between this world and the world beyond is bridged and how a growing harmonization of heaven and earth, a wondrous spring-dialogue between above and below was inaugurated.

In the middle between spring's beginnings and the start of summer, Ascension is the Festival of the Elements. For the elements form earth under the protection of the higher worlds, under the patronage of heaven. We, on the other hand, having become used to direct our sight merely to the outer surface of nature's processes, have to reawaken the sense for the way heaven constantly communicates with earth through the elements.

The elements accompany the year's course with their play. As long as winter reigns, everything on earth is in the true sense of the word 'earth.' Everything tends towards the solid element, the formed and crystalline. Even water, when it freezes, relinquishes its flowing movement and becomes mineral. But when spring arrives, brooks run, rivers flow and sap rises. The watery element begins to rule, freeing what had solidified. It becomes obvious that the earth is a living being. It not only has a body but streaming life. And when in the middle of spring, summer sends out its first emissaries, the accent of all development moves towards the third element, air, which assumes a magically new, creative liveliness. The fourth element begins to be effective in its approach. As summer's warmth, it penetrates everything. But to begin with, it starts out to be active in veiled form and mysterious restraint. But in so doing, it allows the fire out of starry heights to enter, the fire which the Greeks called *empyreum*, the heaven of fire. The beckoning call of cosmic warmth pervades the atmosphere. Likewise, it reaches the watery element. And now there commences a creative exchange between air and humidity. Water, called upward by the rays of the sun, the messengers of cosmic warmth, begins its ascension. Through its union with air, clouds originate. And clouds are the divine sign of this moment between spring and summer.

In the cloud, between earth and fire, between depths of earth and heavenly heights, the sphere of a mobile balance manifests. And at the same time, it is the primal image of metamorphosis, of the organic forming and transforming blessed by the heights. We can be stimulated by looking up at the clouds — be they radiantly white cumulus-clouds or even grey rain-clouds — never to stagnate but to strive instead with upward vision towards the eternal metamorphosis, the never-resting developing!

Between spring and summer, nature is rich in signs and images of the earth-soul's ascension. Among them, the miracle of clouds takes first place. The jubilant soaring of the lark adds the melody. A celebration of high flight, the sense of arising spreads all around us. And in the play of the elements, fire always has the first word in the essential dialogue between heights and depths of the heavens. From above resounds the fiery word and the lower elements follow the creative call with the joy and beauty of ascent.

*

During the time before and after Ascension, the earth becomes the main character in a mystery-drama, in which we can decipher the steps and rules of a soul-drama that concerns us. Earth possesses a body, soul, and spirit just as we do. All that is solid, the element 'earth,' is her body. In fluidity streams her life. The element that inscribes spring's wondrous signs into the heavens with the rising humidity is her breath in which weaves her soul. And the warmth that from cosmic heights calls the elements allows us to sense the spirit that belongs to earth.

The drama begins with the earth-body's attempt to draw life and soul into itself and fetter them there. That is what it does throughout autumn and winter. Earth's life and soul could be cramped and hardened in the physical element. But then, from above, warmth intervenes and, through the fire-element, the spirit of the heights tears away life and soul from the spell of imprisonment in matter. When water and air follow the call of warmth, we experience the body-free earth-soul in our feeling. We behold it in the image of the clouds that speak to us of the living balance between body and spirit. Earth passes through an initiation. The clouds that originate above her and bear her soul up towards heaven turn into earth's sense organs for the super-earthly spheres.

Earth would love to look into heaven; through the clouds she lets arise, she can do so. But then the up-lifted earth-soul has the desire to whisper to the depths what she has perceived, so that celestial secrets might exist on earth. Again the clouds must serve her. They transmit to the depths below what the earth-soul wishes to say. On earth, one then says, 'It's raining,' or 'Dew is falling.' In this way, the earth-soul whispers to earth how the latter can best allow her flowers to bloom, her fruits to ripen, namely, in accordance with the archetypal images that exist up in heaven. For this reason, blossoms and fruits are in reality not products of earth but heavenly forms filled with earthly substance. Herein, above all, lies the secret of ripening that continues throughout late spring and summer until the beginning of autumn.

Spring nature's mystery-play in the macrocosm is a symbol for a corresponding loosening and consecration process in the human being, the microcosm. It would like to be mirrored in man. In the human being too, the four elements, the solid, the fluid, the air and the warmth of blood are bearers of the four-foldness of body, life, soul and spirit. But natural man actually finds himself in a constant winter-condition: life and soul are bound in him to the body as if they were frozen into it. We are so deeply and tightly positioned in our body that, more than we often would care to admit, our body rules over our soul. It like-wise holds fast to our life forces, which are supposed to main-tain our health with their streaming, and brings them to a halt. The reason for the tragic imprisonment in the body, which we human beings experience in this age, is that we know nothing of the spirit's fire. We do harbour it in the warmth of our blood but we do not relate it to the heights of the spirit whence it orig-inates. Through the fiery call of the spirit that man could hear within his innermost being, his heart and blood circulation, he could thaw in springlike manner and enter upon an upward movement as does the earth when, in spring, the cosmic fire conjures forth and inscribes the wondrous signs of the clouds onto heaven. The human life forces could be borne upward as well in the creative ascent, when the spirit, now no longer the body, reigns over them. Between depths of body and heights of spirit, the mobile balance, which possesses the sovereignty of constant forming and transforming, could lend wings to the enlivened soul, the ensouled life. What is made manifest in wondrously symbolic ways in the radiantly white cumulus-cloud could find its ascension-correspondence in the human being. Then, the human soul could join the earth-soul's ascen-sion through the winged movement by which she tears herself away from earth's gravity.

*

As in the macrocosmic, so in the microcosmic mystery drama too, the upward-striving soul could reach the point of acquiring the fiery gifts of the heights, to awaken to the images and sounds of heaven. How this occurs can be deciphered most clearly through the experiences by the disciples who reach the gifts of Whitsun after the forty days following Easter and the passage through the secret of Ascension. Here, the scriptures of the New Testament likewise speak of the elements, namely the cloud and the flames. But neither the cloud that took away the Resurrected One from the vision of the disciples' souls nor the fiery flames that descended ten days later on each one of them belonged to outer nature. In them, the inner human correspondence to the elemental realms is revealed. The hearts of the disciples burnt in longing love for the one whom they lost twice — in the physical body through the Cross on Golgotha and in the Easterly spirit-form when the cloud enveloped their souls like a veil after the forty days. But then the fire of the spirit answered from above to this, their human fire. From within, the fire of the heart burst through the disciples' closed-off state of mind; the sphere of the spirit in which their own higher self hovered above them, found entry into their inner being. The 'fiery tongues' were not just a new source of warmth. It was not a condition of translation and ecstasy that overcame them. The flames were the wellspring of a new light. Their souls became capable of gently seeing and hearing the true nature of the world. Because heaven had opened for them, they heard and proclaimed the heavenly words.

The spark of the Whitsun-miracle, owing to which the disciples rose beyond the sphere of the cloud to the heavenly fire, continued quietly but in a remarkably powerful way through the centuries of early Christian life. Aside from the 'Baptism with Water,' which was carried out as the conclusion of the preparatory purification on those who wished to become Christians, the 'Baptism with Fire and the Holy Spirit' was cultivated. The first readied a person to become a pure vessel. The second made it possible to receive the higher, heavenly content into the soul. The spirit-baptism arose out of the fiery process of Christ-love and faith, when, through the soul-spiritual kindling of the warmth in the human heart and blood, the Resurrected One was not just pictured but actually beheld and experienced as indwelling in such a person. This spirit-baptism was not brought about by the laying-on of hands. The latter only blessed and affirmed the process which had inwardly already occurred. And far into the first centuries of Christian development, the souls gained a delicate vision and awareness for the world of the supersensory through the power of this faith. The cloud of Ascension bore its fruits of flame.

The future of Christianity depends on whether the angelic prophecy is fulfilled, which was conveyed to the disciples when, forty days after Easter, the cloud concealed the unique miracle of the Easter encounters:

'Even as he now disappeared for you into the spheres of heaven, so will he become visible to your souls from there in due time.' [EB]

The cloud spreads between Ascension and the Second Coming; it is the bridge that spans the time between the two. The Resurrected One does not depart from earth after those forty days; he does not disappear in a heavenly sphere beyond. The cloud is the symbol for the kingdom of the elements. He unites with this sphere which flows and breathes through the earthly realm. He only vanishes for the souls of the disciples because they are blind to that world and cannot see it. But ten days later, the fiery seed of a future vision begins to stir. When this vision, which in the form of a grace-filled indication of what was to come, belonged among the miracles of early Christendom, matures in humanity as a whole by means of the appearance of the fervent seed of 'true faith,' then the cloud, the sphere of the elements, meaning, the dimension of the etheric and astral earth-circumference, will become the site where the curtain tears apart. Initially, the 'curtain' caused the miracle-radiance of Easter to vanish for the disciples but then 'Christ will come on the clouds of heaven.'

Whitsun: Festival of the Future

The Whitsun-festival is not bestowed on us by nature. It must be uncovered out of the innermost reaches of our soul. It is *the festival of the future,* for the Holy Spirit, which we hope touch us at Whitsun, is always that which is not yet in existence. It is that which must ever come into existence through a new act of creation. Properly speaking, the Holy Spirit *is* the future. This is the reason why we still have to grow up towards the point of properly celebrating the Whitsun festival. We must mature towards the blowing of the Holy Spirit. For Whitsun is the festival of our true higher self, which as yet only hovers above us. At the same time, it is the festival of community, but not the one that emerges from human intimacies but the one that arises through the harmonizing of our higher selves that are one in Christ.

Whitsun is the esoteric festival of Christianity, the festival of the secret still in concealment. In all honesty we have to admit that while Christianity's outer tradition has always known of the Whitsun festival, any fulfilment of the Whitsun-concept was possible only far from busy external circumstances. Only obscure, quiet groups, who never came out publicly with what they experienced, have rightfully been able to speak of the Holy Spirit. Of course, there were sects that spoke of the Holy Spirit, but their pronouncements were only caricatures of what lived within the quiet mystic, esoteric circles of Christendom. In the Middle Ages, far removed from the mundane world, the brotherhood of the

Holy Grail knew the nature of the Holy Spirit. They knew what it signifies when the dove descends on the sacred chalice. They experienced it; it touched and filled their souls as a higher, indeed the actual reality.

But what does it mean to say that the experience of the Holy Spirit has always been the content of esoteric Christianity? It means that the celebration of Whitsun is not something for beginners but presupposes properly prepared souls. It applies to those souls who are already advanced in prayer and a meditative life.

Even during the very first Whitsun, fifty days after the morning of Easter, what had existed until then in regard to the Messiah conception combined with the disciples' experience through mighty and mysterious destiny-dispensations of Providence. The disciples were not alone during the events of Ascension and Whitsun morning. They were both guests and hosts in the midst of a larger brotherhood of people from the Essene Order. They were the Quiet Ones in the Land, who had made it their task to keep the eternal lamp burning through intense and never-ceasing prayer until the Messiah would arrive. This they did, so that at least this one spark from the light of paradise would endure, that it would not be utterly dark night when humanity's longing would reach fulfilment.

In the religion of the Old Covenant existed a *pilgrimage of the multitudes.* Many thousands of people travelled up to Jerusalem from the neighbouring lands for the Passover festival. The Temple was the goal of their pilgrimage. Thus, the Golgotha-event occurred at the moment when this mighty outer pilgrimage reached its culmination. But in addition, there existed the *esoteric pilgrimage of the few.* Their goal was not the Temple but the house of the Essene Order erected above the tomb of David on peaceful Mount Zion. The festive gathering of those who came from many countries as delegates of the 'Quiet Ones in the Land' reached its culmination fifty days

after Easter on the morning of the ancient, sacred Whitsun festival. The Essene brothers from everywhere gathered earlier to
prepare themselves by means of a sacred ten days. And to
begin these ten days, they went together to the top of the
Mount of Olives.

When, forty days after Easter, the disciples of Jesus went with
the multitude for this festival to the summit of the hill, they still
appeared to be guests of the Essenes. But in reality, all at once
they became the hosts. The miracle of the forty days, during
which time they had experienced the presence of the
Resurrected one in their midst in the room of the Last Supper,
now continued in the open under the sky. Now, the fruit of the
Messianic meditative efforts ripened in the Whitsun-pilgrims
whom the disciples had joined: together they beheld the Lord in
bright glory. The miracle of Ascension became manifest which
Paul refers to when he says that the Resurrected One had
appeared to five hundred brethren at once (1Cor.15). It was
Christ who brought about the first expansion of the original circle of disciples. This could take place because there were prepared, advanced individuals on the inner paths, paths on which
human souls could go to meet the longed-for Bearer of
Salvation.

Thus, when the sun rose on the fiftieth day, the disciples were
in the Essenes' circle, the Essenes were in the disciples' circle.
They had conducted the sacred 'night-celebration' in the way
the members of the Order had been accustomed to do it since
ancient times. The Whitsun festival existed outwardly as well:
the people celebrated it as the festival of the first fruits, meaning the first gifts of newly awakening nature. The outer was the
image of the inner: in the esoteric context, Whitsun was the festival of the first fruits of the spirit. One experienced the beginning of a higher soul-condition, the first ignition of the spirit-
spark, as the first ray of the sun broke on that day. Mighty fulfilment blew through the room when, on this occasion, the fiery

spirit-flames blazed forth directly out of the Easter-sun and brought along the experience of the inner presence of the Resurrected One.

*

The miracle of Whitsun morn blossoms forth from that of Ascension as does the flower from the bud. Christ's Ascension does not signify his farewell from this world. He did not disappear into a world beyond like the one where we seek our dead. He had already emerged from there through the Resurrection. We probably comprehend the Ascension-event best through the words that Christ spoke to the disciples when they were well prepared for them: 'I go to the Father. In my Father's house are many mansions. I go to prepare a place for you' (EB). This is a prediction which, for those to whom it applies, is not fulfilled merely after their death. He does not go to the Father so that those who are his might be accepted in the eternal mansions after death. No, in the midst of life he prepares a place for them where the many mansion of God are. He does this by his Ascension. Through it, he does not distance himself but increases and consolidates his presence.

What does he refer to when he speaks of the Father? The Father is that mighty, all-embracing, all-supportive, blessing Being; all creatures and likewise all hierarchical beings from the Angels up to the Cherubim and Seraphim are limbs on his corporeality. The whole sense-and spirit-world are His body and his soul. He is the Father of us all. But humanity find themselves in a tragically separated condition from the Father. The mighty split passed through creation. On earth, we humans do turn into ego-beings, and attain a certain detachment and independence. Yet our true higher self is with the Father, not with us. A rift has come about between heaven and earth through the tragic developments that ensued from the Fall. The same rift that separates earth and heaven divides human beings as well. All oppression, bitterness and hindrances of earth-existence are due to it. This basically is the truth which the Old Testament places in the foreground: that God is separated from humanity by an abyss. But the reason for this is that humans are separated from their higher self. Their true being is in God. Our earthly being stands before closed doors.

What happened forty days after Easter was that the Resurrected One in his spirit-body, which was becoming more radiant and stronger, grew beyond this abyss. When he says, 'I go to the Father,' this means he does what humans cannot do as a consequence of the Fall. He crosses over the abyss with the human condition he took along through death. Thus he paves the path to the Father for the human soul. He builds the bridge over the abyss between heaven and earth, between earthly man and true spirit man, and thus between man and God.

Christ's Ascension in fact marks the moment when the saying, 'I and the Father are one,' began to be true in the fullest sense of the word. We see this illustrated in art history, for example, in that, starting at a certain point in time, Christ was depicted in the image of the Father. The man, Jesus of Nazareth, did not look the way he is represented in most paintings of Christ. The bearded Christ-image is not a reproduction of how he looked when he walked on this earth. It is an imagination of the fact that the Son and the Father became one. The Son assumes the features of the Father. This is the mystery of Ascension. From then on, when we turn to Christ, we come to the Father, and with that we enter the sphere where our own true self is present.

*

It is thus a Pentecostal theme to speak of the ascension of man. We humans are now allowed to follow the tracks of the one who

has ascended to heaven; a path up to the heights has been prepared that we can henceforth tread. There, we grow wings. For
this to happen we must let the ground of our soul become
warm. Just as air only rises when it becomes warm, so it is with
our inner being. If our soul does not become warm and animated, it does not rise. And prayer is the means of warming the inmost essence of soul in order that the soul can carry out its own
ascension. Here, it is neither the type of prayer consisting of
mere words from the head — it does not warm the soul's
ground — nor is it the kind of prayer into which all sorts of
wishes and desires from the will's region make one appeal 'for
something.' Solely and purely through prayer *from the heart*,
from the feeling human nature, can the soul's very being become warm and animated. This is the form of prayer in which
we aks for nothing whatsoever and set out solely on the path to
the Father. Then the heart becomes warm and the warmth allows our soul to ascend to where our true self exists. The soul's
union with the spirit then comes to pass and only in this way
does man's being become complete. The ego we possess, which
is merely the shell of an ego, is filled with the higher self as its
true content. Thus we approach that sphere out of which the
flames of Whitsun descended upon the disciples.

On the one hand, the Whitsun-flames have warmth, on the
other hand, they possess light. Their warmth must arise out of
human hearts like a fire. Then the Spirit responds out of the
sphere of the Father, where Christ and the Father are now one.
The light-flame of the Spirit sinks down upon the warmth-
flame of the praying heart. The light-flame from above answers
to the warmth-flame from below. Only when we have actively
striven with sufficient patience and endurance to become
warm, may we hope for illumination. Becoming warm is our
task, then illumination is the answer from heaven. The recipro-
cal gift for the Ascension-efforts by the human soul is the gift of
Pentecost. As the gifts of light from a higher realm come

towards us, Whitsun expands into the world. Now, thinking can change and with that the whole activity of human life, which today is formed so utterly out of the intellectual forces. Everyday thinking proceeds from the brain. It moves superficially over external objects and remains fettered to the physical realm. Why? Because man does not think on his own. He denies his own thinking the inner creativity he owes to it. To be clever, bright and to calculate things does not require creativity. It all originates from the brain, more noticeably in one person, less in another. But once *the human being* thinks and not just his brain and cleverness, then the Holy Spirit joins such thinking, for then the true higher self thinks in man. Still, to begin with, without the Christ's Grace of Ascension, this higher self is separated from us. Christ's Grace of Ascension will in future bestow on us a new thinking. Thus, a new culture can finally come into being from the breath that touches us out of the Spirit of Pentecost.

Holy Spirit — Healing Spirit

The festival of Whitsun is a serious admonition every year, all its radiance notwithstanding. It illuminates a mystery that Christendom has so far neglected to realize. On Good Friday and Easter, we recall the mighty, objective *renewal of existence* that came about through the Event of Golgotha. The meaning of Whitsun, on the other hand, is the *renewal of consciousness* that must be brought about by us humans on our own. We work on the fulfilment of this task if we apply Easter's God-given power to sanctify and Christianize humanity's cultural life and our thinking that extends even to the pursuits of science.

*

'Holy Spirit' existed at the beginning of humanity's earthly evolution. Through the Christ-impulse it can and should exist in a new sense as we look towards the future. What is 'holy' is whole. In the paradisal, primal beginning, world and man were still whole. As yet, the separating, wounding tear between creator and creation, heaven and earth, and spirit and substance did not exist. The Madonna-like open human soul was still instrument of divine thinking and will and thus a vessel of the Holy Spirit.

But then the tear of separation broke creation asunder because man, who desired to think and cognize *on his own*, ate of the Tree of Knowledge. Man and earth not only fell from the state of being embedded in the womb of the deity, he even separated from his own higher self which, borne by the Holy Spirit, remained hovering above him. Less and less could it send its effects into the human being who increasingly became cut off and isolated. When man ate of the Tree of Knowledge, he lost the Tree of Life. 'The wages of sin are death.' Above all, man's gradually awakening thinking and perceiving increasingly absorbed death. It ceased to be open in Madonna-like fashion to the spirit. It became more human and masculine. The path led from Holy Spirit to unholy spirit and finally to the spirit-devoid condition of our days. How can the spirit in the human being turn once again to the Holy Spirit?

*

When, in the ninth century, Eastern and Western Christendom split apart, the reason was that East and West could no longer come to an agreement about the nature of the Holy Spirit. It became evident at that time, how far the human spirit had moved away from the Holy Spirit. In cases of theological disputes and discussions it does not make much sense to ask which side is right and which is wrong. The very fact of the controversy shows the uncertainty and the loss of insight on both sides.

In the fourth century, the first classic uncertainty in Christian knowledge had come to the fore and made it obvious that the Grace-filled sureness of primal Christian wisdom was on the point of extinction. The theologians Arius and Athanasius argued whether Christ was more God or man.

In the ninth century, the uncertainty concerning the Holy Spirit was added to that concerning Christ. Eastern Christendom objected most fervently to the word *filio- que,* which western theologians had inserted in the part of the Creed that deals with the Holy Spirit. The East wanted to cling to the original wording which stated that the Holy Spirit proceeds only from the Father. With the term *filioque*, 'and from the Son,' the West groped for that spirituality which, through the Christ Event, had for the first time entered the world. The East's attitude can be explained by the fact that, there, humanity was still rich in ancient spirituality, a spirituality that had been bestowed in ancient paradisal times as divine sustenance for the earthly journey. Like a dense cloud, a common, pre-individual spirit-substance hovered there over the souls who were still open to the Spirit. People did not wish to part from this spirit-substance, because owing to it one still possessed a profound emotional comprehension for the mysteries of Christianity. Having gone farther on the journey through the wasteland and impoverishment of spirit, the West dimly felt that, through Christ's Incarnation, Death and Resurrection, a new spirit fount must have opened up, the gifts of which could benefit humans who were maturing towards selfhood.

Yet, in the same ninth century, a third uncertainty tragically joined the previous two, namely, the uncertainty over the human being. Regarding the question of whether man consists of body, soul and spirit or merely of body and soul, the Eighth Ecumenical Council, which convened in Con- stantinople but was conducted by western theologians in ad 869, decided against the Trinitarian conception of man and denied him an individual spirit-nature. A relative truth is at the basis of this ominous determination: in consequence of 'sin,' the true spiritual self is *not* in man, it merely hovers above him. But because of this it does not belong to him any less and is supposed to move into him if he unites with Christ.

Through the dogma of 869, the West once more lost what it had groped for with the word *filioque*. If no individual spirit-segment belongs to man, how could the new Holy Spirit, brought into the world by Christ, the Son, enter him? Despite the word, *filioque*, in favour of which the West had abandoned its connection with the East, the whole of western cultural and

scientific development — not least of all through the influence
of Arabism — did in fact draw from the decreasing and pro-
fanced stream of the *old* Spirit which originally proceeded from
the Father. The Christian impulse did not influence developing
western thinking, but moved on in its own direction. The side-
by side developments which by necessity turned into developments opposing each other, were sanctioned by any number of
theories about the necessary separation between faith and
knowledge.

*

The seed for the political East-West problem that threatens humanity like a nightmare lies in the division between the Eastern
and Western Churches over the 'uncertainty concerning the
Spirit.' It started on religious and ecumenical ground. Today it
has arrived in the arena of political tension over power. The East
still draws from the ancient pre-individual spirituality, which
by now is directed exclusively to earthly concerns. With final
clever efforts, the collective principle is brought to bear against
the individual one. We speak of the freedom of the individual in
the West. But by saying so, we move on uncertain ground because, extending all the way to atomic science, we have had to
subscribe to a soulless thinking alien to man, a thinking that remained outside the Christian impulse.

Where is the middle between the dangerous power-concen-
trations in East and West? Where is the spiritual Europe, where
is Christianity? Anything torn apart and ailing due to spiritual
reasons in turn can only be healed by spiritual impulses. This is
true to a particularly significant degree of the great wound on
the body of humanity, the schism and abyss between West and
East. Only a Christianity that struggles through to the decisive
Whitsun-ascent, a Christianity that, while it knows well the
mystery of the ancient Holy Spirit, lives above all with the new

Christian Holy Spirit and bravely strives for a fundamental renewal of thinking, of world perspective and science, can build the bridge across the abyss and find ways for healing the wound.

*

When in the ninth century, the great rift opened between the Churches, there existed — far from the outside world and considered heretical by the Church — quiet, little-known groups around the Holy Grail. Here profound certainty concerning the Holy Spirit prevailed. When the sacred chalice was lifted up, the members of the circle experienced the descent of the dove of the spirit upon the chalice with the same certainty with which they experienced earthly visible processes. And in so far as the mysteries of the Grail are the mysteries of the human blood and heart, all their experiences were of an individual nature in the most intimate sense. The stage of the miracle was the innermost centre of the human personality. The chalice, which, when it lit up, had a healing, nourishing and inspiring effect, represented the human heart. The miracle took place inasmuch as the power of Christ's blood came alive in the human blood. Here, the new spirit-fount streamed; here, Christendom came into its own in the Pentecostal sense.

The tragic fate of the Church in the ninth century has turned today into the catastrophic fate of nations and humanity. Could it not be possible for a Christian stream — its low profile notwithstanding — renewed as it is along the lines of the Grail movement, a Christian stream that continues in a modern way what then was only possible in obscurity and concealment, to bring down the healing remedy from heaven and thus to fulfil the mission of the European middle?

*

In the Letters of the New Testament, particularly where plain human greetings are conveyed, it becomes evident that the Christians in the first congregations called themselves 'saints.' 'Give greetings to all the saints among you!' How could that come about when the basic attitude of the Old Testament still lingered on which held that only the Lord is holy? It goes without saying that something more than moral perfection was meant. By receiving the spirit-baptism or the baptism with fire, the first Christians felt filled and ensouled by the streams of the new Holy Spirit that proceeded from Christ. In the beginning, the Father sent the Spirit. But humanity used up and ruined these provisions. When they became critically short, the Father, who had once sent the Spirit, sent the Son. And now Christ sends the new Spirit.

When the fiery tongues descended upon the disciples on Whitsun morning, this bestowal of Grace, apportioned as it was to humanity, by no means came upon them merely from outside without their having had a hand in it. The love of Christ which, following the loss of Good Friday and Ascension, now truly blazed forth in the souls of the disciples along with the amazed awakening that brought belated comprehension and cognition. This love worked like a fire that from within melted away the hard sheathing covering the human being, thus opening the portal to the higher self which, in the sphere of the Holy Spirit, hovered above in longing. Within their own being, the disciples rediscovered the One whom they had lost outwardly. To an unimaginable degree, they thus came into their own. Along with the Resurrected One, their own true 'I' moved into them.

The miracle of Whitsun morn increased and became complete at the noon-hour of Damascus. Here too, what happened came not from without. It was in no way simply an overwhelming spirit-figure that stepped into Paul's path and caused him to fall to the ground. In his Letter to the Galatians, Paul himself described what he had experienced as an event that

took place in his inner being: 'When it pleased God to reveal his
Son in me ...' (EB). As an advanced Whitsun event, Damascus
demonstrates how closely the two fundamental Christian mysteries are related and united: 'Christ in us,' and 'the pouring out
of the Holy Spirit.'

*

Whitsun was made possible only on the basis of Easter. The
Spirit-event emerged from the Son-event. In the Resurrection of
Christ, the 'sovereignty of spirit over matter,' the most sublime
goal for the directions taken by human lives, manifested fully
for the first time. The Christ-ego had moved into the rigidified
human form, separated as it was from God and the sphere of
the Holy Spirit. He had fully penetrated and transformed the
sheaths of soul, body and blood. Christ Jesus was not only the
divine being who had become man, he was moreover the first
complete human being. Jesus of Nazareth experienced the
Pauline principle, 'Not I, but Christ in me' in unique greatness
and wholeness. Spirit not only hovered over him; it penetrated
him through and through. The sickness of sin to which human
nature is fettered and which places man under the spell of death
was healed in him through the fire of the Spirit. Resurrection
was the highest intensification of this healing. The Resurrected
One showed himself to those who had become his own in the
spirit-corporeality which had been wrested from the human
sheaths through the victory over death.

The significance of Whitsun and Damascus is inherent in the
fact that henceforth, at least in germinal form, the transforming
indwelling and sovereignty of the Spirit became effective in
other human beings, something that in peerless greatness had
been attained in Jesus of Nazareth for all mankind.

Through the baptism of the Spirit, the miracle of spirit-com-
munication and spirit-sovereignty continued on to the first

Christians. This baptism was not brought about from outside. The 'act of faith' took place as a fiery process in the hearts of humans. Through it, the cognizing, longing-filled love for Christ turned into Christ's indwelling in the human soul; this then became linked with the entry of the Holy, Healing Spirit, that, from within, can become master over matter. Thus, in early Christendom, the dogma proclaimed in 869 was repudiated in advance. The human being who is merely body and soul, meaning, a fragment so long as his spirit-member merely hovers above him, became complete. Only the Christian who is Christian in the sense of early Christianity is a whole human being.

The wondrous healings that belonged among the miracles of early Christian community life quite certainly did not occur from without. The laying-on of hands, carried out on the sick by persons gifted with a special spirit-permeation of soul, were connected to the laying-on of hands that once had concluded and blessed the spirit-baptism of these individuals. Thus, the Christ-fire of that inner new beginning was rekindled and lived again in the soul of the ill person. When healing resulted, it took place from within as the spirit-fruit of the living Christ-indwelling.

As the gospels recount, even when Jesus of Nazareth said to those who had been healed: 'Your faith has helped you,' this meant: Not I, the human form that stands before you, has healed you, but the higher power that could fill your heart through the act of your faith. This is indeed how it was in the congregations of early Christendom.

*

The act of faith is the inner Grail-process. Artists like Richard Wagner have understood it much more directly than theologians. When the sacred chalice is lifted up in the castle of the

Grail and begins to glow, then the words: 'Faith lives, the dove hovers,' resound. The dove of the Spirit descends upon the human heart aglow in faith, and the heart's grail sends healing, nourishing, enlightening effects into one's own being and into the human and natural environs.

We celebrate Whitsun in the right way when, as modern humans, we strive in a manner befitting the modern age for a fulfilment of the Spirit-mysteries which, like a premonition and foretaste, shone forth once in early Christendom and the context of the Grail. Thinking in particular requires healing by the Spirit. As long as only the brain thinks, the reign of the lifeless, of death, spreads out evermore. When the spirit-part of man moves through the Grail's fire into the human being and likewise into human thinking, the Easter and Whitsun garden of a new living culture begins to bud and blossom.

Healing Through the Spirit

Pentecost is an ancient festival. Most likely, it belongs among mankind's oldest festivals. For us, on the other hand, it is a festival of the future into which we have yet to grow. In particular, we have yet to wrest from it its *Christian* content, its Christ-content. Actually, the widely held opinion among Christians is that along with Good Friday and Easter the mighty drama of the Redemption through Christ has been concluded. While Whitsun does still follow, Christ is not mentioned in the report of the Whitsun event. He does not even appear to the disciples in the form in which he showed himself to them during the forty days after Easter. Something seems to be happening that is not directly connected with Christ. And the connection is a most intimate one. When, as Christians, we speak of the Holy Spirit, we no longer deal with something general as was the case in the centuries and millennia prior to Christianity, times in which human beings even then revered the Holy Spirit. By reason of the Mystery of Golgotha, there exists a *new* Holy Spirit. Christ sends it; the outpouring of the Holy Spirit on the fiftieth day after Easter is the culmination of the stations of the Christ-events.

Not until Christ had died on the Cross and had risen again on the third day, did the divine being turned man arrive completely and fully in earth existence. The healing that heaven had wished to bestow on earth had come. But of what benefit could a magically offered recovery be for humanity if the individual

human being could not acquire it? Following the arrival of
Christ in earth existence, the Whitsun event signifies his arrival
in man's individual existence. When a person is sick and from
the doctor receives medication, then what good does it do to
place it on the bedside table? The patient must ingest the medicine. This was the case on the world-scale. Healing was available but now those who are in need of the medication have to
take it. The first humans who were given this opportunity by
destiny were those who were gathered together on the fiftieth
day after Easter in the Cenacle in Jerusalem.

*

What does it signify from then on to comprehend the mystery
of the Holy Spirit *anew* in the Christian sense? The first thing is
that we can call the Holy Spirit the *Healing* Spirit as well:
'Through him, can the Healing Spirit work.'

In Christian tradition, people were quite familiar with the
healing nature of the Holy Spirit on an emotional level. In former times hospitals were often named 'Holy-Spirit-hospitals,'
because one sensed a connection between the Holy Spirit and
the Healing Spirit. So, a man who does not possess the Holy
Spirit in a way that allows him to receive it into himself is sick
and must go to the hospital, where he at least hopes to find
outward healing.

It can signify a step towards a new Christ-comprehension to
understand the connection between salvation and healing.
When Christ, the Healer, is called 'Saviour' this initially means
that he brings Salvation. But this salvation begins to effect healing when the mystery of the Holy Spirit is added to that of the
Son, meaning, when Christ awakens the Healing Spirit in the
human soul. When Christ can move into the individual human
soul, when it becomes a reality that human beings can say:
Christ in me, then, with that, begins the healing power of the

Holy Spirit. The Whitsun event was the *birth of Christ in us* and along with that the enlivening and kindling of the Spirit's healing power.

Between Easter and Whitsun, the work of Salvation continues on; in the fifty days, the mystery of healing prevails. Out of the mystery of *transubstantiation,* which has come into being through the Easter event, there now also shines forth the secret of *healing,* and with it the maturing of the process of 'Christ in us.' Thus, the motif of healing appears in the Act of Consecration's seasonal Epistles from Easter to Whitsun. Easterly warmth transforms the pulse beat of the heart to 'rejoicing, healing power.' Even the gently beginning Whitsun flame awakens the presentiment of a healing force. What is healed? This is fully and clearly expressed by the Whitsun text: the Spirit whom Christ sends into our hearts is the universal physician who heals the weakness of soul and with it humanity's illnesses. In Greek, illness is called *asthéneia,* meaning, weakness. The Greek language still views the cause of physical illness as a 'weakness of soul.' It is not some outward illness that is healed. It is the condition under which man as such is placed. It is not *any one* illness; it is *the* illness that proceeds from inner weakness. This came classically to expression earlier in the weeks of Easter. The power, sensed to be the one that is approaching, heals 'the self in the depths of the soul.' This alludes to a profound and at the same time completely modern secret: the healing of the ego in the soul's ground.

What is the 'healing of the ego'? We humans travel on our life's path. If we have not become dull and insensitive to the true values of the world, we would like to evolve inwardly. To do this we not only work outwardly but develop inwardly — we battle with our earthly nature. Will we successfully prevail over nature and thus become an individual, an 'I,' in the true sense?

Expressing it differently: we have within us much that we

have brought with us that is not part of us ourselves. We must acquire it, digest and bring order to it until we can say 'I' to it. Initially, it buzzes around in us. Initially, we are not readily master over it. For what buzzes around there? Normally, we think that what has been brought along is primarily what is effective in us through heritage. And it is evident that some hereditary dispositions are causes of illnesses. But what has been inherited is only part of what has been brought along. We bear so much at the bottom of our soul that does not live in our consciousness because we have forgotten it. How much have we experienced and forgotten even if we are still young! In the first three years of our life, we have had infinite experiences that have eluded our consciousness from the very start, because at that time our faculty of memory had not yet awakened. As a swarming hive, all that has been experienced but then forgotten in our present earthly life buzzes around in us. Contradictory matters, even mutually excluding ones are contained there that can be brought into harmony only with difficulty. But when we were born, we did not instantly originate. We came from the prenatal world. What we experienced there for long periods of time likewise belongs to what we have brought along. To this is added what we bring along from former lives, something that eludes our awareness completely. And we are faced with the unheard-of task to permeate all this with the imprint of our 'I.'

We need not bring along anything evil from a previous existence to face difficulties in life. Even the good that we bring along cannot produce good effects to start with without further ado, because it is in disorder. Many of life's trials are caused by the fact that while we bring along much that is good, we cannot achieve harmony within heart and mind.

Humans struggle to become ego-beings, to become themselves. Yet they usually can only grasp a few of the deeply submerged contents and by doing so they repress any number of other matters. And if the striving for ego-awareness assumes the form of egocentricity, then still more is repressed. Then we say 'No' to matters that we love, purely out of contrariety. What a disorder that creates in souls! So we can recognize that a superficial ego-impulse, an as yet unattained ego-striving, makes the disorder complete.

*

In our age, through the focus on the ego's fundamental tendency towards affliction, psychoanalysis has emerged. It points out immense numbers of complexes present in man's subconscious and believes it can help him achieve a certain recovery by calling to mind this or that forgotten complex. But this consciousness which allows a person to think that something totally forgotten happened once and now stirs around in him as a cause of the illness from which he suffers so severely, such a consciousness can in the long run only create greater inner chaos. This could only be avoided if it were possible to impart to a person a total awareness of what they have brought along. But this is just what the ordinary form of psychoanalysis is unable to achieve. Instead of a *psycho-analysis*, we need a *psycho-synthesis*. Bits and pieces of an analysis of the thousandfold treasure that we bear within us, a treasure, however, that contains so much difficulty and tragedy, cannot truly help. It is necessary to forge the whole into a unity, to give it order and harmonize it. But we do not attain an all-encompassing consciousness with the weak mirroring in our heads that we call consciousness today. There we remain in the domain of what we must call the lower ego. This ego grows up and in some way or other has to cope with the innumerable aspects of what we have been born with. It cannot manage them. Formerly, before they became ego-beings, humans likewise possessed a great variety of complexes and components but everything remained less rigid. By nature, human beings could be peaceful and generous. Since the ego has awakened in humanity, there is no more peace; the same goes for the faculty of love of which the still childlike humans availed themselves. In the depths of each soul, in a manner of speaking, a battle of all things against all is waged.

We can comprehend the meaning of the Whitsun event from this vantage point, an event that has occurred for the sake of the ego in man. Through the Christ-effect, the higher ego is aroused in the soul. That higher 'I' does not come to the fore from the sum of the complexes. It is added from above. It descends upon the human being like a fiery tongue. It is the structuring flame of order which forges into harmony all the multifarious impulses that clash with each other and do not want to be brought into unison. Already, the first presentiments of the higher ego pass through humanity. Wherever Christianity is inwardly taken seriously, especially the secret of 'Not I, but Christ in me,' beginnings of a harmony occur inwardly, a harmony not given naturally but acquired through efforts in union with the Christ impulse in the soul. The words of Christ in the Gospel of John indicate this secret: 'Peace I leave with you, my peace I give to you.' The harmony that still remains from the time prior to ego-development, the peace that humans possessed naturally is no longer taken from them, because Christ adds *his* peace, the peace out of the true 'I,' the power of the loving kindness of soul that originates through the Whitsun-flame.

*

Let us imagine ourselves in the circle of those who were bearers of the Pentecostal event. Formerly, what a quick-tempered, impulsive man Peter was! In a mature manner, he can now be speaker for the others. In him, who earlier still remained in the sleep of Gethsemane, the transformation, the healing of the ego has been prepared during the forty days. Now Christ is within him as the fiery flame; the Holy Spirit loosens his tongue.

We witness the miracle of the threefold Whitsun-event: when the storm blows in, we see the awakening of souls. The still dream-enveloped, sleeping souls of the disciples wake up. They find liberation of *consciousness*, liberation of thought. Then follows the miracle of speech, the liberation of the *word*. As in a mighty, universally human confession, the disciples' tongues are loosened, the miracle of speech is fulfilled. It is liberation of soul through the liberated word. Finally, the fiery tongues appear — liberation of the *heart* and blood: the ordering power of the Holy Spirit moves on the paths of warmth into the human soul.

May every Whitsun festival that we celebrate signify a step in the direction of acquiring the Spirit that heals the 'I' in the grounds of the soul.

Between Whitsun and St John's Tide

During the days of the summer-solstice, we move through the golden summit of the year. In her mighty breaths, earth has fully exhaled. She has completely grown beyond herself. She has become so large that her soul is no longer merely down here on earth but above in the heavens. Even as we humans in sleep and, then too in dying, grow beyond our earthly dwelling and move out of it, so does earth in midsummer. She attains to her heights; she touches the Father of the World. Like a mantle, she bears the Father Spirit in the surroundings of her body. On the opposite side of the year, when, instead of the *heights* of summer, we speak of the *depths* of winter, the earth has entirely inhaled her soul; she is completely within herself and from the far distances must receive the blessing of the Father God. In the depth of winter, we therefore have on earth Spirit-pervaded matter, Spirit in substance. During high summer, we have matter-pervaded Spirit, earth's substance lifted up into Spirit.

Man today has become the mighty obstructer. He brings it about that the earth no longer can carry out her breathing in and breathing out in divine manner as was once the case. Once, he too was a cosmic being and in harmony joined in with the Earth's inhaling and exhaling. When, in ancient times, the earth in midsummer grew beyond herself in soul, man grew along with her. He was outside himself. The summer-solstice traditions that were celebrated on mountain tops around fires,

expressed the ecstatic withdrawal of the human soul in
midsummer. Man and the way in which he still lived and
breathed in complete unison, in step with the great cosmos,
was embodied archetypically in *one* figure, in John the Baptist.
He was the greatest, the most mature one in the bodily defined
destiny of humanity in antiquity. For if his date of birth fell in
the days of the summer-solstice, this signifies that he had
shared the period of development in the womb with the
ascending sun during the year. Thus, his being had been deter-
mined through cosmic growth. He was always greater than
what was perceived of his human form with physical eyes.
Through his attitude of soul, he remained permanently in the
condition of midsummer when the soul touches heaven and
man bears the Father spirit 'in the surroundings of his body.'
Those, therefore, whom the Baptist addressed, confronted a
mysterious, mighty human. As a compilation of ancient, cos-
mically gifted humanity, John possessed the natural faculty of
ecsatsy, literally, a state of being out of the body. In this regard
he was the opposite of Jesus of Nazareth whose birthday falls
in the time of the winter solstice. In the stable in Bethlehem, a
boy was born who spent his embryonic development along
with the waning sun, with earth existence's withdrawal into
herself. He was the human being who was to embody the other
universal principle in the most archetypal, purest way, namely,
that earthly man can turn himself into the vessel of a higher
indwelling, literally coming into the body. John, the ancient
cosmic human being, embodies the principle of rapture, of
ecstasy. Jesus of Nazareth, the new earthly man, embodies the
human who is small but can become great if he accepts the
Christ-ego into his human ego.

   In two ways, John the Baptist was the greatest and last
prophet. He knew that the old was ending; that the human
being no longer grew inwardly along with midsummer, but
instead began to dry up and wither. He saw the end of man's

closeness to God and heaven, something naturally bestowed on ancient mankind. And the prophecy of impending disaster that his vision beheld, he put into the words: 'Even now the axe is laid to the root of the tree.' He envisioned the fall of the world-tree. But likewise he knew that now something else was coming: he was simultaneously the prophet of what had drawn quite close, namely, the new Messianic life. He knew that the ancient universal principle of naturally given ecstasy had to yield to the new universal principle that appeared in Christ. It had to yield to the growth within man's innermost centre through a new divine content. Therefore, John said: 'I must decrease,' (John 3:30) — he who by nature carried inner growing within himself. And, 'He must increase' — he who did *not* carry the principle of natural growth and increase in himself. From then on, the summer solstice-fire of ecstatic celebration on the hill-tops turned into the fire of sacrifice. The fire of ecstasy began to be the symbol of that fire in which the old Adam is incinerated so that the new Adam can grow.

But the Christian festival of St John's Day must yet be born. All to easily we remain stuck in the ancient midsummer mood. In future time, the Christian festival of St John's Day will be a great, uplifting festival that will lead us once more to cosmic dimensions. But to do so, we must start at the beginning. If the traditional St John's Day is observed today, one no longer celebrates the culmination of the year; one already enters the beginning decrease of the year's mighty cosmic heights. This is why it is particularly important to bear in mind that in the case of the St John festival we deal with a festive-period, not a one-day festival. For four weeks, the altar in The Christian Community is covered in white, but already these four weeks are a segment of the darkening part of the year. We already face the 'waning' inasmuch as, having left the summit, we once again approach the valleys and lowlands of existence. If in our age we want to renew the St John's festival or establish it properly in the first place, we must not leap to the seemingly obvious conclusion that St John's, as the festival of outside nature, returns its cosmic quality to Christianity. The festival that accomplishes that is Ascension, for there we focus upon the Christ-nature and how it becomes linked to the whole cosmos of the earth. While St John's Day does occur at the culmination of cosmic unfolding, it has significance and inner meaning in that it takes leave of mere nature and turns back again to the quiet of inner human nature. How are we to understand this?

*

During the weeks of the St John's Tide, we call to mind all those scenes with the figure of John the Baptist. A complete drama is played out before us. Let us just follow the course of the first of the three years of Christ's life on earth for a few moments. On January 6, John baptized the one in the Jordan in whom, unlike the others in whom exctasy was brought about by baptism, the mighty indwelling of the Christ-ego in human nature took place for the first time. John himself was the guide who led from the ancient world principle over to the new one. When, on the other occasions, he submerged those who were to be baptized in the waters of the Jordan, he brought about in them what took place naturally in the human being during midsummer, namely, a moving-out from confining housing. But in the one whom John baptized now, the great miracle occurred: the Christ-being, the lofty Sun-spirit, moved into the wide-open soul of Jesus of Nazareth and assumed human form. The greatest man of ancient humanity handed over the baton of world history to a new age. He himself helped the new to enter. He was able to bid farewell to ancient greatness embodied in him. He did not cling to it. A patient humanity can now pass through a zero hour and find their way to new greatness.

Following the Baptism in the Jordan, Jesus of Nazareth found his first disciples among the followers of John the Baptist. They had formerly been the Baptist's disciples. The latter still stands in the foreground, but soon the great sacrificial journey begins: the sacrifice that John carries out inwardly is reflected outwardly when he is thrown into prison. Are those who were his disciples supposed to take his place? Even Jesus of Nazareth still remains in the background. But at Whitsun of the same year, through a new call to discipleship, Jesus gathers those who had made a connection to him while still with John the Baptist. A community forms that prepares for what is to come. And then the profoundly tragic shadow falls upon the stage of the drama: on August 29 — according to tradition — the Baptist is beheaded and the gruesome plate with his head is carried into the hall where Herod celebrates his festival.

This was the signal to seek completely new directions. Now Jesus sends the disciples in pairs out into the world. He himself withdraws into seclusion. For half a year the disciples are on their way and experience a miracle. They experience John the Baptist, who has fallen victim to his enemies, as their constant companion on their journeys, their patron saint, the angel above them and the entity who unites them in true community. The seed of a Christian, ecclesiastic community and, along with that, Christian Church is finally formed through the experiences of the disciples during this time before they return to Christ.

In the Feeding of the Five-thousand, it becomes particularly evident how John the Baptist has turned into the angel who with mighty wings hovers over the nascent community. Its wondrous magic spreads out prophetically over human beings of the future. This not only applies to the circle of the apostles; the five-thousand are the symbol of that future humanity who will be part of this new principle of community. John the Baptist prepared the way for the Other so that he could enter earthly incarnation. John continues to remain the one who prepares his way. Inasmuch as human beings accept Christ into their souls, a new growth can commence. The shrunken, diminished, ego-endowed human receives the seed of new greatness. The ancient cosmic greatness of John will one day re-arise as human beings learn to grow beyond their own confines by means of Christ's indwelling them. But that greatness will not merely be personal greatness. To begin with, a transitional level will be constituted in human beings so that man can grow into true spirit-community. The new cosmos is not immediately ready and complete for mankind. The germinal beginning of a new cosmos originates in a new community of human beings.

The secret of the 'three years' unfolds. And when the years 31 and 32 are over, the Golgotha-hour of decision has taken place and the mystery of Christ's death and resurrection has occurred, the possibility has been implanted into earth's depths to receive a new heavenly height. The remarkable encounters of the disciples with the Resurrected One intensify to the event of Ascension forty days after Easter. Christ extends his existence, he begins to grow. Now John's words are fulfilled: 'He must increase,' Ascension is the entry, the growing of the Christ-entity into the whole cosmic environment of the earth. And if human beings henceforth accept Christ into themselves, it likewise makes it possible for them to grow beyond the confines of selfhood and once more to turn into cosmic human beings.

To start with, Ascension is followed by Whitsun. In the disciples, a new ego-centre is developed through their love of Christ, their pain of loosing him and through their ardent efforts to remain close to him. The higher ego that shines forth in them through Christ's indwelling them is the centre in each individual from where the Christ-sphere can expand. Directly on Whitsun-morn, the disciples have furthermore experienced that along with the new selfhood, the new Whitsun-ego, the first indication of community is present. When the higher 'I' awakens in man, the accord is there, regardless of whether one knows the other or not. Over all the world, one is a member of his body. The dome of the true Church arches over all those who in their souls make room for the true 'I' in that they sense the redeeming power of Christ. The perception of the new world-encompassing range together with the awakening of a new higher energy in their very own centre of being evokes enthusiasm and the certainty of a mighty sense of a mission in the disciples on Whitsun morn. They feel how the Holy Spirit gives them strength not to think of themselves but to work in the world for something great and whole. The apostolic charge of every Christian human being begins at that hour.

*

From Christmas, we followed earth's ascending life. In fully unfolded spring on Ascension Day blossoming forth out of Easter's joy, we have sensed the new cosmos originating through Christ. Finally, the Whitsun festival moves us forward to the summer solstice and up to the full height of the year. There is good reason already at Whitsun for thinking of John the Baptist as the one who prepares the way for Christ.

What step is Christ taking now that we can follow? It is the step from the individual spirit-filled human being to the Grace of the spirit-filled community. John the Baptist is the guardian genius of the growing community. In the future, it will be understood why St John's festival frequently follows a short time after the Whitsun festival. The more we are able to turn the Christian festivals into cultural events instead of merely attractive ideas, that is, to celebrate them a way that emanates a stronger and more powerful mood, than for instance the sensations of sports-events, we will get to know the more wondrous triad of Ascension, Whitsun and St John's Tide.

Ascension: the Resurrected One transforms the ancient cosmos by uniting with it into the new cosmos.

Whitsun: by feeling the Resurrected One within himself, man attains the ability to unite with the new cosmos. The mystery of the new community that overshadows him is for him the beginning of the new cosmos.

St John's Day: John the Baptist, the representative of the old cosmos, leads to the new cosmos as the protective genius of the community.

Christ has moved into earth's whole circumference. Man discovers the Pentecostal germinating centre, the Christ-filled, Christ-blessed ego, within himself. And the genius above our heads, who protects and strengthens the Christ-seed in us, is even now moving his wings. And as we experience the miracle of community under his wings, this miracle becomes for us the passage-way for entering upon a brotherly relationship with the whole cosmos, all living creatures, with earth, sun, moon and stars. Then Christianity will expand; it will cease to be an insignificant personal matter *apart* from cultural life. Rather, it will become the truly decisive factor, even though it is not evaluated by statistics, large numbers and outward successes but remains in obscurity.

From year to year we must be mindful to gain ever more from St John's time and to allow it to become more fruitful. A beginning for this is when we realize how closely related the two sayings are: the Pauline one, 'Not I, but Christ in me,' and the words John the Baptist spoke: 'He must increase, I must decrease.' Not I, Christ in me, — and inasmuch as Christ grows in us and if, by inner unselfishness, we make room for this growth, he bestows on us the breadth of true community and beyond it a new cosmic frame of mind. In so far as humans have lost the connection with the cosmos, they disturb the rhythm of the seasons and do not know that it is they who turn everything into chaos. But to the extent that the Christ-mysteries grow in our souls and our congregations, not only will healing of what personally afflicts and worries us but likewise the healing of the cosmos emerge from such a state of soul. What proceeds from our altars will be a medicine for the world, a remedy for the destructive, disease-causing influences that issue from humans, influences to which all creatures, and particularly man, are constantly exposed to nowadays.

Summer Solstice

At midsummer the earth's soul becomes pious. The warmth that flames through the atmosphere is like a mighty sacrificial fire on the wings of which the soul soars upwards towards the sun. As the soul of our planet holds communion with herself during midwinter in mighty cosmic contemplation, so she grows reverently beyond herself at the height of summer. She praises the heights of the universe, uniting herself with her upward-rising hymn of flames.

In ancient times, the earth's soul-condition was in harmony and unison with the exaltations of piety in men's souls. The devout of antiquity knew and sought for their gods in the height of the cosmos. To be lifted and borne up to the gods beyond all of earth's gravity was their fervent longing. This was why ecstasy, rapture, was the characteristic of the pre-Christian religions. Religious life in the times of paganism was kindred to summer. No wonder that among all the celebrations of the year the summer solstice was the most outstanding festival. The earth-soul's macrocosmic ecstasy swept human beings up to the microcosmic ecstasy of their jubilant hearts.

The summer-related ecstasy of ancient cosmic piety has wrongly been rejected as being contradictory to Christianity. It was a form of Christianity prior to Christendom. For the deity to which men lifted their souls in longing was none other than the Christ-being who in those times was still connected with the sun as the heart of the cosmos. Only when, for the sake of humanity, Christ departed the sun's heights in order to become man on earth and to unite himself with the sufferings and depths of earth, the piety that sought sun-rapture found emptiness. From the very beginning, Christianity quite rightly distanced itself from all ecstatic elements, for henceforth Christ was united with the earth and could only be found here. So long as a reminiscence of knowledge still existed that Christ had descended from the sun, Christianity retained a cosmic breath. But when the connection between Christ and the sun, still understood by early Christendom, had been forgotten, the Christian religion shed its cosmic character and its supporters turned zealously against all 'pagan' ways.

The last herald and bearer of ecstatic sun-greatness was John the Baptist. Not only through his birth, but through his whole being, he was the man of the summer solstice, the very embodiment of superhuman cosmic rapture. His flaming soul, ablaze far and wide over the land, flared up to the heights of the sun just as Christ departed from these heights and made ready to tread earthly paths together with men. John was allowed to accompany the genius of the sun from the heights to the depths by carrying out the baptism on Jesus of Nazareth. He understood the mighty transition and change in the spiritual universe and selflessly reconciled himself to it. This induced him to utter the solstice-words: 'He must increase, I must decrease' (John 3:30).

The growth of Christ, henceforth proceeding from the earth, of which the Baptist speaks and before which he steps back, replaces the principle of rapture. A new soul-inclination for ascent thereby comes into the world. No longer does man lose himself in a deity beyond. Rather, he now truly finds himself for the first time and penetrates to his own higher being inasmuch as he makes room for the divine indwelling, the 'Christ in me.' The festival of St John's Day at the midsummer's solstice will in future be more than a festival of remembrance of the Baptist as

the last bearer of ancient cosmic greatness who was ready to
'decrease.' It will be a special festival of Christ's increase. Christ,
the lofty sun-spirit, has moved into the breath of the earth. In the
souls of humans who allow him to dwell in themselves, he constantly grows. He grows rhythmically along with the earth's
soul in the changing of the seasons, following the breathing in
until the depths of winter at Christmas, then rising with the
earth's breathing out towards the sun until midsummer and St
John's Day. The summer solstice brings about the union and harmony between inner and cosmic ascension. In the summer solstice, Christ instructs us out of earth's nature, with which he
united himself. He teaches us a new *sursum corda*, the heart's
sense of ascent. And through the new Christian renewal of the St
John-experience, Christianity is given back its cosmic character,
the quality that spans the heights and widths of the universe.

From Pagan Summer Solstice to Christian St John's Tide

Summer Solstice! This word points to the highest intensification of the pre-Christian religious mood. The great pagan nature-religions culminated in the ecstatic midsummer-jubilation. These celebrations continued on to later centuries when fires were lit on mountain tops and around the fires circle dances were performed and songs were sung, because the ascending human soul sought a connection with the earth-soul that had risen up high. This is why, in St John's Tide, the Christian summer festival, paganism and Christendom reached out to each other. But how can the pagan midsummer-ecstasy be transformed to the Christian era and changed into Christian piety?

Nature culminates during the summer solstice. It reaches its moment of greatest unfolding. More than at any other time of the year we are drawn into the breath and pulse beat, into the whole sphere of nature. It is philistine to think that the earth is indeed covered in midsummer with more verdant growth of vegetation, but otherwise it is the same as in spring or fall. Our feeling allows us to sense something else. It tells us that earth during the summer solstice is larger. Everywhere, it has grown beyond itself. Not its mineral body, but its soul expands enormously. When spring arrives, the earth-soul begins to grow; it tries its wings and slowly sweeps upward. In so doing, it has the first encounters with what comes towards it from heaven.

And when the profusion of blossoms that adorn our earth so colourfully, has fallen once more to the ground, the earth's soul grows and ascends still further. Earth outdoes itself in its dimension. During the longest days of the year its soul-growth culminates, becoming one with the whole cosmos. In midsummer, we need not look up to sun or stars so as to experience the cosmos; no, the earth itself is the cosmos. The great totality surrounds us here and now.

Earth's condition of rapture-filled expansion to highest heavenly heights is actually a return by our planet to its primal beginning. During the other seasons of the year, too, earth is surrounded by the air's sphere and in the atmosphere by the remarkable cycle of ascending and descending water that becomes visible in the clouds. Thus it has always been evident that the earth is larger than its solid rocks. If one were to measure its size, one would have to include at least the layer of air. Why? All that is fluid in the earth's circumference, becomes visible in the clouds, sparkles in the morning in the pearls of dew on the meadows, streams down in rain — the watery sheath of earth — is a memory of a cosmic primal time when earth was much larger than it is today, because it was still fluid and as yet not hardened into the solid mineral form.

The 'earth formed out of water' that is mentioned in the Letter of Peter in the New Testament (2Pet.3:5) was still united with the moon in one cosmic body. The sheath of air as such is a memory of a yet older aeon when the earth was *still* much larger, for it had not even congealed to the degree of fluid density but was aeriform. The 'air-earth' was still one with the sun. Now, in midsummer, the earth grows upwards and out of the cosmos a mantle of warmth comes to meet it. The summer's warmth-sheath of our planet is a memory of its very first primal beginnings, the Saturnian primal beginnings, a condition still known to Greek philosophers like Heraclitus, namely, that everything existing originated out of fire. The reason that summer's warmth points to such cosmic universality is because it is a reminiscence of the primal beginnings of time, when earth was still the whole cosmos and not yet crystallized out of the latter like a single drop. This cosmos was a warmth-cosmos. In midsummer's nature, we experience a momentary return of earth-existence to its beginning out of the fire-element. This makes the earth so large. The earth's soul then reaches up to the fire-heaven which the Greeks called *empyreum*.

Earth is a mighty living being. We have to participate in this living being's breath and life-rhythms. If we really do this, we recognize in summer earth has entered a condition akin to sleep in the human being. In winter, earth is awake, it has completely withdrawn into itself. It falls asleep when spring passes over to summer, just as we fall asleep in the evening and are then no longer in our senses, because we expand with our soul-spiritual being beyond our body. When we sleep, our body is like a garden where fresh life sprouts and grows so that the following morning we are restored once more ready for the decomposition-processes of the day. Thus earth is renewed in summer when it annually falls asleep. The fiery heights of the cosmos bestow new strength on earth: primal earth touches our present earth.

*

In history, figures stand out in whom we can observe a correspondence to the summer's earth-ecstasy, humans who grow beyond merely human measure to superhuman measure as does the earth in summer beyond earthly dimension. The last of these superhumans was John the Baptist. If we picture him living in the desert covered in animal skins and only eating the simplest food, we do not focus on the essential part of his nature. That is expressed in the fact that his soul extended greatly beyond his body.

Eight hundred years earlier, there lived another who likewise possessed an atmospheric quality and carried the whole cosmos, as it were, within himself, because with his soul and spirit he transcended his bodily being, namely, the Prophet Elijah. The simple man who spoke to people on occasion as the Prophet Elijah — his biblical name was Naboth — did not distinguish himself from other men. This is why people in general did not know that Naboth and Elijah were one and the same. But his opponent, Queen Jezebel, knew quite well why she ordered the stoning of Naboth. She wished to destroy Elijah. But when that simple man who owned the vineyard proceeded to speak as the messenger of God, he no longer was Naboth. Something like a mighty thundercloud surrounded him. Then he was a whole atmosphere and people in far-off regions saw and heard him even though he was not in their physical vicinity.

John the Baptist was similar. His activity as the herald of Christ did not merely consist in calling humans in such rousing terms to repent. His activity that brought the land far and wide to feverish excitement was due rather to the superhuman, the atmospheric quality of his being. It was like a mantle of warmth. One might regard figures like Elijah and John the Baptist as walking flames. It is well known that the greatest heat of a candle flame begins where the visible light of the candle ceases. The invisible mantle of heat extendds beyond the flame we see. In the same way, earth in summertime resembles a flame that is surrounded by its mantle of warmth; thus, figures like Elijah and John were flames whose region of soul-activity extended like a mantle of warmth over regions far and wide.

Earlier conditions of earth, above all the 'fire-earth,' resound in nature at midsummer. So too, in figures like Elijah and John, an ancient law of human nature re-echoes. If we go back far enough in humanity's evolution — disregarding the trivial view that man is descended from the apes — we reach the point where, as the offspring of the gods, man was far larger than he is today. In the course of ages man shrunk down increasingly to his physical form. The sagas of giants are not mere fairy tales for children. In ancient times, humans were gigantic in soul. The physical bodies were perhaps no larger than they were later on. They were like the visible flame and around it, like the heat-mantle of the candle's flame, was real man. Ultimately, there were individuals who, in accordance with their inner dynamism and significance, were so great that, even though they decreased in size like the rest of humanity, they still remained superhuman. And among these, one towered over all the others, that being who once appeared as Elijah and later as John the Baptist — it is the same one. In him, man of the primal beginning, Adam himself, passes in various forms through humanity's history. He is the super-human man whom we might also call the archetypal father, because originally the human being was so large that he was completely enveloped in the 'Father-Ground of the World,' the Father-Fod. Just as earth was once enveloped in the warmth-mantle of Saturnian primal time, a time that echoes in midsummer's nature, so, too, was man once enveloped in the Father-Being. John the Baptist is the one who, as a last one, bore the mystery of the archetypal father. This is why it says of him in the Gospel: 'among those born of women there has risen no one greater than John the Baptist' (Matt.11:11). Greater is meant here in the sense of soul-space. We can now begin to understand why John the Baptist has been depicted as a bearded giant even though he had to bid the earth farewell while still young, for he was killed at age thirty. But in the short time in which he could do his work — perhaps it was not more than one year — he was like a fire blazing far. He was the archetypal father, the embodiment of earth-ecstasy at the summer's solstice.

It is important to realize that even today we still bear in us the legacy of original greatness, though we have been reduced to the lowest terms in our human nature. We see it in the nature of a child. Although initially it has a small physical body, its life-body which as yet is not fully formed, and, to a greater extent, its soul-sheath are still as large as the world. The child possesses much life, but this is not yet its own life. The life of the world still pulses through it. This is why a child's supersensory form is larger than that of an adult. It has the whole cosmos in the circumference of its body; it resembles the earth in summer, for it has not yet completely left the sphere of its heavenly origin.

We also see it in the nature of sleep, though we simply consider it natural and have become accustomed to sleeping at night. But what actually happens when we fall asleep? It is then, once again, that we expand greatly beyond ourselves. We possess something in our nature that earth's nature makes evident in summer. Because we expand at night into cosmic realms, we are strengthened anew in the morning. In the child and in the sleeping human being, something of the ancient gigantic human nature extends into the scaled-down human. This too is part of the theme of the summer solstice.

*

In recent history we see an enigmatic side of the summer solstice. When the time of midsummer draws near, it is often a time when conflicts erupt somewhere. It could be experienced to a special degree in Europe in 1914 when, in July and August, in the heat of summer, the world was plunged into calamity. Then, out of the chaos of emotions, the war was born which was only the first evocation of all the catastrophes that followed later. A further culmination of these puzzling pattern occurred in 1939 and then 1941. When, following the prohibition of The Christian Community in 1941, we heard in our prison cells that the war was being extended even to the East, it became clear at once: Apocalyptic tragedy in unthought-of proportions would be poured out over humanity.

But what does it mean that such calamity-spreading tempests of destiny erupt out of the blazing heat of midsummer? A similar puzzle is frequently posed by the climate and weather of midsummer. Why is it that it rains throughout a summer or that again and again hailstorms destroy ripening fruits in fields, gardens and on trees?

The extension of ancient world conditions into the present and the activation of old cosmic forces, something that is the signature of the summertime-solstice, increasingly produces a crisis. The ancient forces are no longer viable. Nature alone can no longer help humans to progress, not even the nature of midsummer. The mysteries of the world of antiquity, of human ecstasy and greatness in the superhuman form of such prophet-figures like Elijah and John are no longer the law of the present. But if humanity wishes to cling to the ancient forces and is not willing to let go of what is past, then this very behaviour invites disaster. Through the influence of ancient world conditions, the time of midsummer is predisposed to be the period when the ever-repeating cycle of disasters manifest.

This is not incomprehensible. We shall try to find the reasons for it. What was brought about when the fires were lit on top of the mountains, fires that blazed up into the night-sky while people were given up to jubilant abandon? Not only through the sight of the fire, but above all through the dancing and jumping in the midst of the flying sparks, people tore their souls away from the earth and were thus transported to other spheres. When this was still timely and corresponded to human nature, a revelatory echo answered from the heights into which the souls allowed themselves to be borne up by summer's ecstasy. In the Druid culture, for example in Celtic-Germanic north-western Europe, the inspirations received by the Druid priests streamed down in special abundance. Among others, monuments of this are the great numbers of ancient, impressive megalithic avenues in Brittany. These gigantic processional roadways are often aligned on the summer-solstice sunrise. The solstice was the occasion for receiving the gifts of the gods. And the means for receiving them was ecstasy, intoxication, the process of being torn out of oneself. But being torn out into an ecstatic, out-of-the body state of mind was always at the expense of what we today call wakefulness. One did not become an awake, free and conscious human being. Rather, one received the gifts of the gods while being out of one's self in a dull dream. This is no longer appropriate for the human being.

In *Midsummer-Night's Dream,* Shakespeare describes in the wondrous alternation of human and superhuman scenes where human beings and in turn elemental beings are the actors, how through unconscious midsummer-dream-elements all kinds of fantastic revelations float into people's minds. But the dream of midsummer had to lose its innocence. When the time had come for man to awaken to reasoning consciousness and freedom, the midsummer-night's dream turned into 'midsummer-night's madness,' as it is appropriately called in English. When ecstasy no longer flourishes under the protection of the gods, it has to end in demonized forms. Then, a kind of mental illness arises from the element of intoxication. Through the nature of mid-summer, human souls are swept along into the earth-soul's sleep, even if they do not make any special effort in this regard. The result is that if they do not watch out they sink into dull sleepiness. Rudolf Steiner never tired of pointing out how the outbreak of the First World War has to be traced back to the fact that during those days, in all the countries involved, the leaders were not fully awake. A midsummer-dullness covered their hearts and minds. And because these men were wanting in alertness, the terrible train of events suddenly started to move and could no longer be halted. Since 1914 this has happened again in midsummer only too often. During the most decisive moments, the decisions that were made were not based on wakeful but on demonized thoughts.

The summer-solstice-ecstasy on the hill-tops was always guided by the motto 'I must increase.' Human beings truly grew in soul. In addition, the national factor, nationalism, the exhilaration of being one people and being part of one's own folk-soul were fostered in special measure by the summer-solstice fires. When people were lifted up beyond their own confines, they initially entered into the element of the folk-soul. It is obvious that when the motto 'I must increase,' which is inherent in the midsummer-ecstasy, is experienced in the sense of the folk-soul, it immediately becomes a source of the quest for power, for imperialism. Here, it becomes almost tangible that the forces of the ancient world can no longer be beneficial but can only bring immeasurable harm. A whole series of world-conflagrations are stirred up by what overcomes human beings through the midsummer-mood if they do not take the decisive step of transformation. Something that once was mighty and holy, namely the warmth of midsummer, has turned into the heat of fever. A Christian summer-solstice festival will be like the healing of one who is sick with fever. This is the reason why it is so important now to recast the pagan summer-solstice-festival at long last into the Christian St John's festival.

*

Always and again, it is enlightening when contemplating John the Baptist to see how he, the greatest representative of the ancient world-principle, makes room for and paves the way for the new that has to come. The archetypal father who still bears the greatness of the universal Father around him like a mantle, becomes the herald of the Son. He says: 'He must increase, I must decrease.' In John the Baptist, the superhuman decides to become human; he renounces cosmic greatness in order to condense into the humble human form. The correlation between the two birth-dates emerges in splendid clarity. The summer

solstice is the birthday of John the Baptist who says: 'I must decrease.' The winter solstice is the birthday of Jesus, of whom
John says: 'He must increase.' The man of antiquity hands the
rudder over to a new principle.

The two principles are reflected by the season of the two
birthdays. The nature of John the Baptist, born at the summer
solstice signifies, is akin to the nature of earth at midsummer.
Earth's cosmic greatness is reflected in the superhuman greatness of man. Six months later, at the time of the winter solstice,
the child of the Luke Gospel is born in the stable at Bethlehem.
To begin with, it appears that this one will not be 'great.' There
are many representations from the very early Christian period
where John the Baptist is depicted as a giant and, standing next
to him, quite small, Jesus. In John, a human being was incarnated in whom something of the prenatal condition existed, of the
condition man possesses while he is still in heaven. He was not
completely within his body, but was larger than his body. But in
the one of whom John said, 'He must increase,' an entity was
born that likewise came from heaven but became fully incarnated. He completely entered into the human state; relin-
quished divine greatness and chose human smallness. This was
incarnation to the fullest extent. In him who was born at the
winter solstice, the archetypal son emerges, in whom man himself becomes a creative being. He does not remain enveloped in
the mantle of the Father-God; he completely assumes the
human destiny of smallness, of insignificance. But in this smallness, he develops the Son's power, freedom. The path from John
the Baptist's birthday to the birthday of Jesus is like the path out
of the prenatal realm into incarnation. This is man's actual destiny. Even though fully incarnated man does easily forget that
he originates from heaven, he must pass through the point of
nothingness.

The words of John, 'He must increase but I must decrease'
are ordinarily understood to mean that the one uttering them

wishes to underscore his own unworthiness in penitent self-denigration in the face of a higher one who deserves each and every honour. But they are deeper. Early Christianity recognized a cosmic aspect of these words. While it might appear that the Baptist said something about himself that also applied to the sun — since, beginning with the summer solstice, the sun's power decreases and the days become shorter — yet, in the cosmic sense, the words by the Baptist relate more to earth than to the sun. In John, the earth speaks: 'I must decrease.' After the summer solstice, earth changes. Until then it grew along with summer's ascent. But beginning after the solstice, when the sun recedes, earth again breathes in its soul. And it signifies an awakening for the earth when once more it gathers into itself its ecstatically out-poured soul. Deep sleep in midsummer is now followed by an ever more alert condition. If we read nature's allegory accurately, we realize that in actual fact earth does not become impoverished in autumn and winter. It neither loses that part of itself that was outside during summer and caused it to be so large nor the heavenly blessings and gifts that the cosmic heights bestowed. Rather, earth takes it all within.

When we understand this, we find the connection from the meaning that John's words have for the earth to the meaning they have for man. The human being must make the effort to embody what is of the heavens. We should not become morally smaller, nor constantly criticize ourselves like a schoolmaster. We should rather gather together our human potential and concentrate it in all humility. Then we join in the process that is affirmed by the words of the Baptist as a goal for humankind: 'He must increase, I must decrease.' With all his heavenly wealth, man must fully enter incarnation. When as children we were greater in soul than later on, have we lost all that made up the magic of heaven, the radiance and splendour of childhood? No, it simply has become so ingrained in us that we do not always know right away what to do with it. How would it be if

we were to learn to work with what we have drawn into the
narrow bodily sheath as we age? How would it be if we were to
rediscover and lift the spell cast over our soul's heavenly abundance? Yes, it is truly so: at night when we sleep we are
immense; upon waking, we slip back again into our body. But
we take along what heaven has bestowed on us during the
night. The only problem is that man no longer understands how
to take what he brings along out of the night and make it come
directly alive and fruitful during the day.

Now, what is meant by the saying: 'He must increase'? John
the Baptist does not say it simply in reference to the Christ-
being. Rather, he is referring to the being of Jesus. Let us place
the image of the Baptism in the Jordan before our mind's eye.
There is John the Baptist with his magnificent greatness of soul.
To him comes one born six months later who is completely
human; who has even entered into the bitterness of human destiny, and bitterness causes inner shrinking. He is small, John is
large. But when John baptizes Jesus in the Jordan, Jesus will
grow. Through what? Because the man who has become small
now receives an unheard-of heavenly content. Jesus receives
Christ into his being. This is the beginning of a new law of
greatness. Man cannot retain the ancient greatness which John
the Baptist possesses. He has to become small but then he can
say: 'Not I, but Christ in me.' And when John says, 'Christ must
increase,' we can understand it like this: 'I must decrease, Christ
in me must increase.' Then man grows once more, but it is not
really man who grows but the higher man in the human being.
Christ himself is the law of growth. This is the perspective that
the Christian St John's festival suggests, namely, that greatness
once again moves into the human being. But this is not the
greatness of antiquity, the greatness of the Father. The Son
enters into the son-man.

He who can say, 'Not I, but Christ in me,' is small, humble,
selfless by saying, 'Not I.' But inasmuch as he says, 'Not I, but

Christ in me,' he bears something within himself that is not identical with his earthly, natural human nature and yet can yet blaze
forth like a fire out of himself. When man becomes a
Christophorus, when he becomes small in order to turn into a
bearer of Christ, he becomes once again the conveyor of fire, not
the fire of ecstasy, rupture or intoxication, but the fire of incor-
poration, of wakeful inwardness. And a revelation, a blessing
will likewise respond to this St John's fire. Throughout the
whole year, a summer solstice benediction can take place. Where
this fire burns, one need not wait for the summer solstice.

Today, the fire of the Christ-incorporation brings about the
answers and gifts of heaven. The human being who burns with
the Christ-fire will once again be the inspired human being.
And this must be felt particularly at the St John's Day festival.
First, calming must occur, the 'healing of the one suffering with
fever.' This means that man must be ready to relinquish all that
resembles intoxication, all that has been brought along. 'I must
decrease.' Man must be willing to become small, to turn inward
and concentrate on what he has within himself as waking man.
This is the Johannine turn of the summer solstice: in soul, we
must always be willing to withdraw into ourselves, not to seek
out there in the world for any riches, leisure and distraction.
Then, the words 'I must decrease' also mean, I become concen-
trated. And the St John's turn of the summer solstice can be followed at the beginning of autumn by the Michaelic turn. The
annual festival that is opposite of Easter then receives its content. The storms of autumn may come but the human being
who has gathered inner wealth can utter the words that Rudolf
Steiner gave for the autumn festival: 'Man has been resurrected
and can confidently lay himself in the grave,' for the eternal
human being within is saved by Christ's incarnation.

Then, John and Michael hold a dialogue. After all, the life of
John the Baptist was not at an end when Herodias had him
beheaded. The being of John the Baptist continues on in John,

the Apostle. But in so doing, the archetypal father himself undergoes the change from superhuman's world-greatness to man. The disciple whom Jesus loved, who lay at the breast of Jesus, is completely human. In him, the ecstatic greatness of John the Baptist has turned completely to the inwardness of the disciple, John.

This John embodies the highest level of the human condition, the Spirit-Man, who, through Christ's incarnation, bears the spiritual life completely within his inner being and thereby sets out on a new growth-process. At an advanced age, John the Evangelist and disciple becomes John the Divine on Patmos.

The apocalypse is a dialogue between John and Michael. The apocalyptic inspiration that is gleaned from the Christian St John's Day festival pours forth in fullness and power. The pagan festival of the summer solstice brought inspiration through ecstasy and intoxication; the Christian festival of the summer solstice brings inspiration through innermost con- centration and higher soul-courage. The aged disciple John beholds the trumpets resounding, fire falling from heaven, mixed with hail. If human beings try desperately to cling on to the ancient cosmic forces, only world conflagrations, one after the other, can be enkindled. On the soul-level — and only too often in the outer sense as well — midsummer's heat can become an inter- mittent fever that rages back and forth between fever's heat and hail stones. If humanity struggles through to the new principle, they open up to the golden rain of the heavenly Jerusalem. The priestly vestments of St John's Tide point with golden figures to the new gifts of heaven that are bestowed on the soul that rests in concentration within itself.

St John's Tide in the Year's Rhythm

The summer solstice was always a celebration of the sun and light. The view of the Christian St John's Day festival is likewise aimed at sun and light, but is dependent on penetrating through the senses' shine and arriving at the essential element that speaks to us through sun and light. It is, after all, celebrated when the ecstasy of the longest day and the shortest night are over. Our celebration of St John's Tide is like an *echo* of the solstice as the outer culmination of the year. There is a dep wisdom in this. At one time, June 24, St John's Day, coincided with the summer solstice, but then it moved away from the solstice as a result of the Christian calendar. Today, June 24 therefore occurs three days *after* the summer solstice. People can observe the St John festival in greater composure and freedom once summer's culmination point has passed. In the future, the 'first Sunday after St John's Day,' this will acquire a resonance similar to when spring's 'first Sunday following the full moon in spring.' For even as the full moon in spring is the culmination of what the moon bestows on earth, so, the summer solstice is the greatest intensification of what earth can unfold in it relation to the sun's light and warmth. The culmination points in nature must be awaited; only afterwards can we celebrate the Christian festivals, Easter in spring and St John's Day in summer.

The inner situation of the St John festival is illustrated in a humorous way in Richard Wagner's *Meistersinger* (III.i). It had been a turbulent night, things had been topsy-turvy. It was the night before St John's Day. People were thrashing each other without knowing who the other was. A colourful throng rushes across the stage. And now, when St John's Day dawns in golden stillness, Hans Sachs is sitting in his shoe shop. He is a human reflection of John the Baptist whose name he bears (for Hans comes from Johannes). Once again, he reflects why people are always fighting. Last night had been rather wild, all the fun notwithstanding, quite like on the evening before a wedding.

> Man, woman, apprentice and child
> assault each other as if mindless and blind:
> and if madness allows it,
> it will now rain blows.

He cannot get the sound of the rhythm in which people beat on each other out of his ear, the thrashing continues in the music. But now the clamour has passed and he arrives at the most sympathetic solution of the riddle: the nature of midsummer is at fault.

> A *glow worm* missed its little mate;
> It then caused all the damage.
> The *lilac* did it — St John's night!
> But then came St John's Day!

Oh yes, summer's night! When the lilac blooms — this refers to elder-berries — and when the glow worms flit about, there is magic in the air. When the days are the longest and the nights shortest, fires are lit on hilltops and everybody dances and leaps. People leave all orderliness at home and surrender to the splendid cosmic disorder inherent in summer's ecstasy. But subsequently the gentle fruitful glory of St John's Day must arise.

To discover the *Christian summer* is a task that we will be able to solve only with time. But when the longest day and the exuberant, short night arrives, we are not yet in summer, just at summer's beginning. Summer only comes after midsummer-night's madness, it unfolds *after* the summer solstice. The miraculous abundance of summer, only develops during the descending half of the year. This awareness has disappeared to a large extent, in no small measure due to religious customs and institutions.

The year is a remarkable totality of rhythms. The cosmic background becomes manifest not in numbers that stand still but in rhythms, in the upward and downward surging of a wave. That is the secret of time: it does not move along a straight line, but moves in oscillations, it dances. If humans were not so immobile and boring but would move along with pulsing time, they would know better what being human means. Man is stuck, but time nevertheless pulses. And should not the innermost element in our life, religious striving, also pulsate? If Christendom tries to evolve into the future, it must move along in a living way with the year's rhythm. We must know what it signifies when the festivals fall in the various seasons of the year. At most for the Christmas festival and in case of Easter, a diminishing feeling for the time of the year has still been retained. We have to learn anew how intimately the thought of Christmas is related to the earth-rhythms winter-position and the thought of Easter to spring-position of the earth-rhythm. But above all we need to regain a feeling for the whole year; the empty space that is called the festival-devoid half of the year must be filled out.

It is a one-sidedness that Christian festivals exist in the main merely during the ascending part of the year. At Christmas, the sun begins to ascend again. At Easter time this continues and at Whitsun-tide it still goes on. But for the time when the sun descends during the year, from St John's Tide, summer's beginning, through Michaelmas, autumn's beginning, until Christmas, corresponding Christian contents for the year do not exist. Is it therefore surprising that humanity only likes to acknowledge all that moves upwards but is afraid of what moves downward? But we cannot swing along in the cosmic rhythm if we experience fear of the descent, for example, fear of ageing. The whole of human life today has therefore become a-rhythmical, uniform, lacking in rhythm. How is it with the wondrous rhythm of day and night? Is it still truly experienced as a rhythm? In fact, we merely value daytime, for then we are active. We simply put up with night. But if we do not live in the rhythm of day and night and love both parts, the ascending and the descending one, we will soon no longer receive benefit and blessings from sleep. Night will leave us empty. It will refuse us its secrets and gifts. Then life merely consists of lengths of day-time with gaps in between that are nothing.

Human life likewise represents a rhythm corresponding to the year's course. The middle of life corresponds to the summer solstice. Life today has become deprived of rhythms, without pulsating vitality. This can be clearly discerned by the fact that only in rare cases will people truly continue to develop past mid-life. The ultimate reason for this is that human beings are reluctant to give up the remainders of their youth. They have forgotten that ageing can have great value, namely, when the descending branch begins after mid-life. We go along with it, particularly so long as ageing can still be touched up. Still, we cannot change it. But truly to affirm this part of the wave that does not rise but falls, yet which frees up the inner side of exis-tence that earlier was frequently covered up by the blossoming interior, truly to say 'Yes' to ageing is something that we have yet to learn anew. We never arrive at maturity and fulfilment of our innermost being without this affirmation.

How is it with the most minute rhythm that we constantly activate inasmuch as we breathe in and out? In a world where the meaning for rhythm in all things large and small is extin-guished, does breathing not have to become shallow? Do peo-ple even breathe at all today? Of course, we cannot avoid breathing altogether, it still moves a little. What a wondrous help inhaling and exhaling could be for remaining alive within!

Goethe knew how to express this splendidly in the verses of *West-Östlicher Divan*:

> A twofold benefit comes from breathing:
> Inhaling air and letting it go.
> The first oppresses, the latter refreshes,
> Thus life is blended wondrously.
> So, thank God when He presses you,
> And thank Him when He lets you go.

The whole of life is dominated by rhythm that blends life remarkably. Inhaling presses; exhaling refreshes. The whole of life contains times when we are pressed into ourselves, but there are likewise times when we can once again trust ourselves confidently to life's surges. And what happens to us if this alternation does not take place? In comparison to that, the wife of Lot who turned into a column of salt was still a moving figure. The annual rhythm of spring, summer, fall and winter could above all be the great school within religious life where man would learn to overcome rigidity and all that lacks rhythm, and once more acquire rhythm, the true element of life. The mighty inhaling and exhaling of the earth are the year's seasons. Earth as the great maternal living being breathes out from Christmas until St John's Tide; then breathes in again from St John's until Christmas. In exhaling, we have the Easter festival, the festival of Whitsun, all the way to the summer solstice; in inhaling, the coming-into-its-own, the entering-into one's own inner being that begins at St John's. St John's Day celebrates the start of inhaling; then, at Michaelmas, follows the great station of the intensified coming-into-one's-own. The earth inhales all the way to Christmas: we are completely within ourselves, even as earth is completely within herself.

*

What actually is rhythm? Whether we take the year's rhythm in
the great scheme of things, the rhythm of day and night in the
small scheme of things, or on a still smaller scale human breathing or our pulse beat, in rhythm, the etheric world is revealed.
The physical, material world, visible to our senses, does not
stand still, but swings and lives in rhythms. This is a manifestation of the etheric world, the first sphere, closest to us, of the
supersensory realm. Where rhythm works, we are in touch
with the streaming forces of life and formation. If, as is often the
case today, we no longer have an understanding of the intimate
connection between religious life and the rhythmic element, we
cut off the religious element from that of life and suffer an inner
atrophy and loss of energy. In this lies the tragedy of the development in the last few centuries that humans ultimately wanted only to acknowledge physical-material existence as being
real. But that reality is static and rigid; it bears death within.
The life forces that flow, weave and swing through the world
are invisible to ordinary human eyes. But wherever there is
rhythm, the sphere of life forces becomes manifest. And particularly in religious life, this sphere should once again play a
powerful role.

There is a tendency today, originating in America, to preserve
the physical form. When somebody dies, for instance, they are
embalmed and, with make-up and styled hair are placed in a
chair. The deceased appears at first sight like a living person.
One does not wish to see death and conjures forth a spectral
illusion of life. But this is merely a symptom for the tendency
that emerges out of materialism to want to cling to life and
maintain its physical condition. But by tearing life out of its
rhythm, one surrenders it even more to death's power out of
one's fear of death. Only where death is affirmed as a rhythmic
counter-movement to life, living elements have full access to
man's existence, and human life acquires its true meaning.

The etheric world manifests in rhythm. We can even go farther and see the sun circling in the heavens as the source of all rhythmic aspects in our cosmic system, because it is the source of all life. Modern astronomy calls the sun a 'yellow dwarf,' because, viewing fixed stars as huge cosmic bodies, astronomers believe they have discovered that many among them are significantly larger than the sun. Indiscriminately, the concepts of modern scientific research are applied to the sun. Even though science relies on nothing but hypotheses, it is said that the sun is 'a complex of nuclear fission.' One is not aware that by saying this one describes the sun as the seat of death, the throne of the spirit of death, Ahriman. In reality, if we do not merely consider the physical aspect, the sun is the source and seat of life. Only one who thinks and feels this way can begin to have an idea that the sun and Christ were once closely connect-ed, and that a change occurred in this connection when Christ came to earth in order to become man. With this, a sense can be gained for the fact that along with the incarnation of Christ as man the rhythmic life on earth has received a mysterious new content which henceforth swings along.

The sun on earth, how do we experience it? Now, this is not meant in the physical sense but in the life-bearing, life-giving sense. The sun is actually the primal phenomenon of rhythm. This is why it rises and goes down. This is why it magically con-jures forth the rosy dawn and sunset glow of evening along with day and night. Where is the best location to find the true nature of the sun, at the equator, or in temperate latitudes? If the sun's nature is viewed purely in terms of amounts of light and heat, it would be best to go to the hot desert regions in order to encounter the sun's true nature. But there the sun is fierce like a beast of prey. Life cannot thrive there; only desert remains where the sun can be so totally effective in the physical sense. It is in temperate zones where the blessing of the sun can be best experienced. For the sun can only be comprehended through the rhythmical nature, the etheric nature within itself.

At the equator there is a complete cessation of seasons — the summer solstice reigns there all year long with constantly equally-long days and nights, something we only experience at spring and autumn equinoxes. Nights and days remain the same there. There are no vatiations. Due to the heat of the physical sun, rhythm ceases. By contrast, at the earth's poles, the extreme of the seasons holds sway. For half a year the sun is in the sky without it turning dark, for the other half, it is night without the sun rising.

In the rhythm of temperate latitudes in the middle, it is possible to experience the true nature of the sun: namely the complete rhythm and balance.

*

If we allow the Christian St John's festival to convey its wisdom to us, we understand that it is the festival of the sun, but of the sun that from this time on begins to descend. It is the festival of light, but of that light which now gradually becomes dimmer. We know that as the summer's sun descends it bestows on us the most wonderful fruits. The rising sun allows growth, the descending sun causes ripening. And it possesses this magical power of ripening in late summer and early autumn. Then it bequeaths the finest fruits. Nature herself teaches us to love the slow descent, the downward swing of rhythm. Humans themselves must actively fill their life principally *after* mid-life. What stands in their way here, as has been indicated earlier, is that life today has been separated from the mystery of rhythm. Most people, having apparently reached their goals in society by the age of twenty-eight or thirty, come to an inner standstill. Basically, what follows then is the continuing recurrence of the same thing. Even in the cases of significant outward successes, there are no longer any true developments and breakthroughs to something new. Yet this should be the very time for new beginnings, just as the descending sun allows the best fruits to ripen after the middle of the year.

Christianity has to become cosmic once again. When we say that Christ has united with the earth, this may be hard to comprehend for many people, since they only think of the physical earth. But earth possesses an ether or life body; she has her rhythmic entity. The rhythms in the life of our earth, particularly in the year's course, reveal her etheric elements. Christ has moved into the rhythmic-etheric element of our planet; he can be encountered in his life forces. But these swing to and fro. They exhale from Christmas until St John's Tide; they inhale from St John's Tide until Christmas. In this breathing, this swell, we are allowed to seek Christ. And particularly after the summer solstice, when earth inhales and finally culminating at Christmas, a particularly intimate relationship of humanity to Christ opens up. Along with the mighty in-breathing, Christ makes his entry into the depths of earth-existence. It is this growing approach that is referred to by John the Baptist, who stands at the summit of the year when he says: 'He must increase.' Year after year, an increasing closeness to Christ can be experienced just at the time when the year descends from its height.

Now, John the Baptist could not say: 'I must decrease,' if he did not have something to give. The word of waning alone is proof for the fact that John was one of the very great ones. Only one who has, can give. And one who gives, grows. now one might think: he has given something away, hence he has become less. Certainly, something in John does decrease. But precisely because of that, something else grows in him; we could even say, *another being*. This is connected with the fact that from one year to the next we become more familiar with a mystery. When we say the name of John during the St John's festival, our soul's eye seeks him as an altogether great being — after all, he is called an Angel or messenger of God (Mark 1:2) in the Gospels — we can find him on the level of the Angels. And as the Angel of the Lord he teaches us how to offer up sacrifice, teaches us to pray. In the life of ritual we have a training in which we can learn the art of deepening our experience of rhythm in a new way. The ritual leads us through the rhythmic recurrences into a higher sphere of life. In this school, the of the Angels, the exemplary one who prays and offers up sacrifice, teaches us how, on our part, to say: 'I must decrease, he must increase.' He is the patron, the guardian angel of the ritual, rhythmical, religious experience that sways in the rhythm of the offering.

*

Thus we properly enter into summer in the time when the sun drawss closer. At this very time, spurred on by John the Baptist, we can raise ourselves to the level of the Angels. At Whitsun we found the courage for the ascent to the true human condition, for the flame of the higher self had touched us. We experienced that the human being is allowed to strive for the heights. Now the path is open to strive for that inner height that has as its background the descent of the outer world. Inasmuch as we join the ranks of John, we touch upon the angelic stage. And when the rhythm of the year descends further and autumn begins, we can even raise ourselves to the level of the Archangels. We take the step from the St John's festival to the festival of Michaelmas. During the descending part of the year, man may grow, not physically, but with his inner being, because Christ can grow in him. In the two festivals, St John's Tide of summer, and Michaelmas in autumn, we find the true Christian content for that half of the year which at first sight doees not have Christian festivals. And if we continue to grow, it continues from man, Angel and Archangel to Christ himself at Christmas. John — Michael — Christ, this is the ascent during the descending half of the year.

Transformations of Michael

Is the sun really none other than that shining fireball out there in space which, while it has a gigantic but still measurable radius and size, is circled at an enormous yet measurable distance by our earth? Is it not rather ever-present, hence surrounding us on earth ever so closely, so that the celestial body that circles the sky above us is merely like a sign, an indication of an all-encompassing, all-penetrating being? Is it perhaps the visible heart of a mighty spherical entity which, as such, is not visible to our sight, but in the effects of its forces wishes to be perceived by all the remaining organs of our full human condition? Specially as the life-bestowing power, the sun cannot be identical with that fireball. For if there were nothing but its physical radiation of light and warmth, then only atrophy and death could proceed from it as we observe in earth's desert regions.

The ancient mythical consciousness of humanity still looked through the sun as through a window into a differentiated, hierarchical sphere. The Greeks viewed the sun as the vehicle of a god, the chariot of Helios. But behind and above Helios, they revered a higher, more inclusive deity, Apollo, whom they called Phoebus, the god of the Sun. The sphere of Helios still points to something that our eyes can behold. The sphere of Apollo, on the other hand, is of a supersensory nature. Apollo is the lord of spiritual sunlight and, as bearer of the solar lyre, he is ruler of the divine harmonies of the spheres that have their fount and centre in the sun. As Goethe says in the prologue of *Faust*, 'The sun-orb sings, in emulation, 'mid brother-spheres, his ancient round.'

When the ancients turned to Apollo, they sensed the sun's etheric body that is immeasurable and fills our universe with the pulse beat of its life. Yet, even behind and beyond Apollo, the mysteries of antiquity knew still higher divine entities, higher and highest living members, as it were, of the all-encompassing being, 'Sun.' In the doctrine of the triune sun by the philosopher-emperor, Julian the Apostate, ancient knowledge reverberated into Christian times. After Zara- thustra had once taught about the highest spirit-entity of the sun as Ahura Mazdao, the great sun-aura, it became known as the god who passes through death and resurrection. In later pre-Christian religions that longed for his coming, the devout revered him as Osiris, as Adonis and under numerous other names. Only for a short while, in early Christianity, a faint idea existed that, in Christ, the highest sun-spirit had lived as man among men. In the age of Julian, the Christians had already forgotten this secret.

*

Knowledge of the hierarchical angelic kingdoms was still taken for granted everywhere in the texts of the New Testament. Traced back to Dionysius the Areopagite, the great Athenian disciple of Paul, this knowledge continued into the high Middle Ages in a marvellously structured teaching of the hier-archies. This is a chapter of ancient sun-wisdom that streamed into Christendom. What the ancient world had experienced in direct vision was preserved in human feeling, namely, that the sun is the window through which a very high spirit-being looks down upon us, that from every level of the spirit-worlds it speaks to us through those beings who are its vessels and messengers. Thus, images endured where the hierarchies were seen as arrayed in such colour-filled circles, and together forming the mighty hidden, spiritual sun-aura behind the physical sunlight. Many works of art, for example the mosaics in the cupola of the Baptistery of San Giovanni in Florence, attest to this in later centuries. Not only the kingdoms of the gods look upon us through the eye of the sun; here, we look into the spheres of the heavenly hosts when we penetrate beyond the eternal that dazzles us.

This is why the Archangel Michael plays a special role whenever mention is made of the totality of the angelic hierarchies. In the medieval Legends of the Saints that accompany the year's course day by day, the legend of the Archangel which falls on September 29 contains the enumeration and description of all the nine angelic levels; Michael is in fact designated as Prince of the Hierarchies. For the Archangel Michael is the Archangel of the sun. He appears behind the sense-perceptible light of this celestial body as a spirit-figure that is still relatively near the human level. But he is merely the countenance of higher realms of existence, ultimately that of Christ himself. Behind Michael they all appear, in so far as they are vessels, members of Christ's body and self. Even as the face of a man is not his essential being but only a part of his ensouled bodily garment, although more transparent than the rest of the body so that the self can be revealed through it, so Michael is the countenance of the totality of the hierarchies that belongs to the spiritual world and at the highest level the countenance of Christ.

*

At the culmination point of its dramatic vision, the Apocalypse of John shows us Michael as victor over the dragon. The scene of the battle with the dragon recurs through all stages of humanity's spiritual history as a fundamental mythical image. In

pre-Christian time, we have exalted deities who carry out this
battle with the bestial opponent. In the Babylonian region it is
Marduk, in India, *Indra,* among the Greeks, *Apollo,* who casts
the dragon Python into the Castilian gorge. At the time of early
Christendom, the Persian cult of the divine sun-hero *Mithras*
spreads out over the whole Mediterranean region. In Christian
times we find human heroes who overcome the dragon. In
northern pre-Christian lands, as yet not there is *Siegfried;*
among the saints of early Christendom, *St George.* Is the con-
queror of the monster always the same, merely designated by
different names, be they divine or human? The secret that links
the various conquering figures with each other concerns the
angelic hierarchies on all levels of the spiritual ranks of beings,
triumphant ones appear above the dragon. In Marduk, Indra
and Apollo, entities appear in pre-Christian times who stand
above the level of Archangels in this image. They appear shining through the Michael-figure, as if through a transparency.
Michael, the countenance of God, stands between above and
below. When, at the mid-point of time, the Christ-event took
place, human beings, who through their spiritual power rose
above the general human level, became transparent for the
form of the Archangel Michael who worked through them. For
instance, the last Nordic initiate, Siegfried, and the first
Christian knight, St George are human beings of this magni-
tude. Michael-metamorphoses appear on all the rungs of the
celestial ladder due to the transparency in the realm of the spiritual sun.

*

In the image of the victorious battle with the dragon, we encounter a mystery both of the sun and of the spiritual being of
man. Man owes his erect form that enables him to triumph
over all that is base to the spiritual forces of the sun, just as the

plant has its force of uprightness from the sun. Because man is inwardly sun-related, he rises above the animal which, through the lack of an upright form, remains bound to the forces of earth's depths. Expressed in the simplest terms, the meaning of the mythical image of the battle with the dragon is the overcoming of animal-nature through man. Externally, on the bodily level, this is the evolutionary history of the past. Inwardly, on the soul level, it is the continuous moral goal of the future. Initially, higher divine beings are the victors over the dragon. We observe the sun-forces at work, how they labour on creating the human being throughout mighty cosmic stages.

There are descriptions by Rudolf Steiner that relate the image of Michael's battle with the dragon to the origin of the physical animal kingdom. Spiritual guiding powers were holding man in the spirit realm, awaiting the proper time when humans would be mature enough to enter into an earthly incarnation. These guiding powers had to guard against opposing powers who did not want to wait, prematurely hastening towards incarnation. In a mighty spiritual battle opponents are cast down to earth. Thus, before physically incarnated human beings existed, the dragon-like firstborn of the earthly animal kingdom came about.

On every level of evolution, drawing ever closer to the level of the earthly realm, the battle with the dragon took place. It ended with the casting down of the beast. This always occurred for the protection of the developing spirit-man, who, throughout all lower stages and distortions was to be fashioned after the highest sunlike, divine archetype. Finally, the highest ruler of the sun, who bore the archetype of man in his own being and could therefore be designated as the true man-god, entered into earthly incarnation so as to liberate human beings, who had fallen away from him, from the dragon-forces of the depth.

When, in Christian times, metamorphoses of Michael have emerged as human conquerors of the dragon, we can understand from this that the future of spirit-man, threatened as it is by demonic powers, has now been placed in human hands. Particularly in our apocalyptic present, we must reckon with the *human* sun-warrior. Those meeting the spiritual demands of the time who are servants of Christ are the ones who in the Michaelic sense are Michael's companion-warriors.

Human Beings,
Angels and Archangels

At the beginning to the autumnal season, the being who is called the Archangel Michael in the Old and New Testament was revered since ancient times. But what can the name and the festival of an Archangel signify for the human being with modern-day consciousness? Is there space for Angels and Archangels in the framework of the present world view? Indeed, is there even a spiritual world? In ancient times, the veneration for Michael issued out of world views that still considered the supersensory to be more important than the sensory. These ancient visionary world conceptions have long since been extinguished and lost. Even in the circles that claim to be nurturing the Christian-religious life, people do not want to know anything about a real supersensory world: while the biblical texts are seen as authoritative for everything one thinks and believes, where mention is made of Angels, Archangels and other hierarchical beings that transcend man, one does not go along with the Bible's world view. People are not even fully aware of this inconsistency. But for the modern human being who is conscientious in thinking and speaking and therefore rejects the thoughtless usage of traditional concepts and names, the mere reference to the name of the Archangel Michael is a call to wakefulness. Such a name can be mentioned honestly only if a breach has been made in the wall of that world view denying

spiritual hierarchical beings. Much less can we undertake to celebrate a Christian festival in Michael's name, if we do not admit
that a new world view is dawning that makes it possible again
for clearly thinking modern humans to be convinced of the existence of Angels, Archangels, Seraphim and Cherubim.

Just to speak consciously of an Archangel signifies sounding
a Michaelic tone, a sound of courage that pierces through the
walled-in materialistic image of the world and overcomes the
half-truths and inconsistencies of traditional, religious thinking.
The world does not stop with man, the true world only begins
beyond the human kingdom.

Since ancient times, September 29 was not merely dedicated
to Michael as a single figure. It was the day of looking up to the
totality of the heavenly hierarchies. The Archangel presents
himself, as it were, as the banner-bearer who strides ahead of all
the 'heavenly hosts.' For this reason, on the day of Michael, the
old legends of the Saints always preface the story of the battle
against the dragon with an enumeration of the nine angelic
hierarchies. From spring until the end of summer, outer nature
has borne man. When autumn begins, outer nature abandons
him. Man has to turn from outer to inner. He finds the strength
for this if he knows that he enters a whole new world in his
inner being: the sense world dims, the supersensory world tries
to dawn within the human soul. Inasmuch as Michael helps
man to cross over the threshold of autumn, he directs him
towards the world of the hierarchies that henceforth will
replace for him the world of the natural kingdoms.

*

What would it be like if the prevalent scientific world were
right, if only the world of senses existed? Such a world would
be condemned to sterility, to utter barrenness. In the framework
of existence grasped by the senses, everything would only go

round in circles. There would only be variations within this prison-like, spell-bound domain. Something new would not enter in. Inescapably, all existence would move towards the moment when the energies of our solar system will have been exhausted, the limited resources would produce no more energies and all would perish in heat-death of the universe. As cooled-down slag, our world would collapse into the abyss.

If the world with its four kingdoms came to an end, if there existed no world beyond the human being, what would happen, for example, with our dead? No possibility of thought for their existence would remain. A final extinction would be the last breath. Likewise, the world of the unborn would not exist. Nothing would be left except the trivial and actually completely estranged view of thinking that dominates as dogma in the churches, namely, that man with his whole being originates through conception and birth. Birth and death would be walled-up doors behind which there would be nothing. But the spheres of the unborn and departed intermingle with the spheres of the Angels and Archangels, the hierarchical beings above us.

There is still more. An essential constituent of human life would be negated along with the negation of higher worlds, namely, sleep. Today, people view sleep merely as our nightly habitual, regular interruption with no content of its own. It can only be understood as fulfilling and fruitfully affecting man, if an insight is acquired that when we go to sleep, with soul and spirit we leave our body and, though unconsciously, move into the sphere of the higher entities, the same realm into which the spheres of the dead and the unborn are likewise woven. How much has it impoverished our life that we no longer grasp the miracle of sleep and the night! One who merely focuses on man's daytime nature, meaning the meagre sum of consciousness that we produce during the day, knows only a tiny fragment of man. Man is truly much more than what today's manner of thinking knows of him. Just sleep alone is proof of this. In the nights, we live and breathe together with the angels, the souls of the unborn and our dead in a higher world, even if the minds of scholars deny it ever so vehemently.

Finally, and this is important above all, if there were no world above man, no ideals would exist that man can strive for. There would be no development and no real future. The course of time would be no different from a tightly sealed room with a ventilator running that is supposed to create the illusion of fresh air for the occupants, while in reality merely the used-up air is being recirculated. Just as no ideals would endure, higher forces would not exist that could benefit human energy. The abstract thought of 'God' that alone has remained from ancient world conceptions, conceptions that still knew the living elements of supersensory worlds, cannot fill the gap. Not until one no longer shies away from speaking of a 'divine world' will the holy word 'God' signify something again for humanity.

The basic reason why man would be doomed in his inner-most efforts to fruitlessness, fatigue and failure if there were no world above him is that our own higher being, our true self, does itself still belong to the world above us. Only little of the actual human being is realized within us. The most important potential still hovers above us. This, our higher self, is the one that causes ideals to shine into our soul. An image of what we are to become is more or less clearly borne by us in our soul, because again and again we sense our own higher being that is not within but above ourselves. Borne by Angels and Archangels, still resting in the womb of a higher world, there is our true self. There, where the dead and the unborn are, to where we unconsciously ascend when we sleep at night, we are with that part of our being that extends beyond our earthly sheaths. In reality, we deny ourselves when we deny the exis-tence of the Angels, Archangels and higher hierarchical beings.

*

All this gives us a key for finding our way as modern human beings to the truth of the hierarchical worlds above us. We must not think that beyond man, an insurmountable chasm exists that divides us from the deity. The entities above us are not distant. The chasm exists, and is hard to surmount. But it is important to see how the angelic realms work in a vital way into human existence everywhere. We as human beings are intimately related through our higher nature to Angels, Archangels and to higher beings. The reason is because, in the course of the aeons of world evolution, Angels and all the other hierarchical beings once passed through the human stage. On earth, during the earth-aeon, *we* are the humans. During the aeons preceding the earth-aeon, Angels and Archangels were on the level of humans, even though they bore no similarity to the image of man today. They have continued on and in each aeon have developed in themselves one of the higher members of being which man will unfold in later aeons. The future of the human being is the present in Angels and Archangels. An Angel is advanced by one aeon from man, an Archangel by two. The Angel possesses as reality the next higher member of being to which man is merely aspiring now and which he views as the distant goal of his ideals. The Archangel has realized a further stage within himself. When as culmination of my inner striving I grasp th dawning of my higher being, at the same moment I am touched by my Angel. And when I learn to unite with my Angel, I fill myself at the same time with my own higher self. I can understand the nature of the Angels and Archangels when I imagine my own higher nature.

Attempts such as these at least to begin to comprehend the relation between man and the angelic worlds, will immediately be countered by the question: how can we speak so simply of man's higher members of being? What is meant by this? The questioner may feel able to understand the idea in general about a higher being that still hovers above us, but feels confused by talk of different members of being into which the higher human nature is divided.

In fact, much stands in the way of a differentiated conception of man's being. We are in the habit of simply calling the physical form that we see walking on earth, 'man,' or 'human being.' But we are not readily aware how subtly man is differentiated in so far as he belongs to the sense world as well as the soul and spirit world.

But we make no progress if our considerations of man do not lead to full, definitive concepts. Rudolf Steiner's anthroposophy has given a key to that. We bear within us the results of three aeons that preceded the earth-aeon. In the first of these aeons we developed the physical body. The next aeon wove into the physical body the second sheath, the life or etheric body, which pulses through this physical body and keeps it alive. A third aeon added a third sheath to body and life, namely, the soul. From then on, man was an ensouled living creature in the earthly realm. But as yet, the soul was not the actual human being. It was merely a sheath, as were the physical and the life body. Only during our earth-aeon, the spiritual human being, the self, has begun to descend into the three sheaths and to incarnate. The significance of the present aeon which we call Earth is that the human being becomes an self-conscious being. Our self already existed during the earlier aeons, but it still hovered above the earthly sheaths, borne by the hierarchies of heaven, even as our higher being still hovers above us, borne by the hierarchies of heaven. We live in a cosmic median of the universe. Three aeons are behind us and thus we bear with us the three sheaths they bestowed on us, the bodily sheath, the life-sheath and the soul-sheath. Like three garments, they take into themselves the actual essence of man's being, the still budding and seedlike self.

In three future aeons, man will incorporate into himself three higher members of his being. His slef will not remain inactive. Rather, it will work on itself and take hold of the sheaths, leading them towards an ongoing transformation. Through the spirit-penetration of these three sheaths in the course of the aeons of creation, man will learn, step by step, to bear within himself the celestial triad of his higher spiritual being.

The first step is not to allow emotions, urges and wishes that pop up to dominate our soul. Instead, out of the centre of our being, we set goals and direction; we establish order and harmony between our soul forces. To the degree that human beings in the future purify their soul-sheath according to the ideals that shine towards them out of the world of their higher being, permeating this soul-body with the traces of spirit, they draw in what we could term the 'higher soul,' the first of our higher members of being. Rudolf Steiner called the latter the 'spirit-self.' It hovers above us, but we can even now foresee it and often we can feel as if we were touching it. At the same time, this spirit-self is the life-element of the Angels, even as the ego is the life-element of the human being. The Angels developed their ego during the last aeon, they are now working on the spirit self. An Angel has the higher soul as his soul around him. And when we strive for our higher soul which hovers above us, we touch the spirit self of our Angel at the same time.

When, in a future stage, man becomes capable not only of harmonizing and purifying the soul through the power of the spirit, but to transform his life-sheath as well, then he will develop that higher member of being that, already today, is the life-element of the Archangels, the 'higher life' which Rudolf Steiner terms 'life spirit.'

When it finally becomes possible — and this is a matter of a far-distant future — for man to exercise the sovereignty of spirit over matter itself, purely out of spiritual power to transform his physical body, then he will gain a share in the life-element of the Archai, the 'Spirits of Personality,' the hierarchy that stands above the Angels and Archangels. This then is 'Spirit Man,' the spirit-body in which man with all his sheaths is utterly and completely identical and irrevocably united.

*

Although it is our task in a future aeon, when earth will have disappeared, to develop the 'higher soul,' or spirit-self, which as yet only hovers above us, we can and must work on our soul even now. We are not *human beings* if we leave the chaos of egoism in us the way it is. Our soul body must become a pure mirror for the best, the purest, the most beautiful that inflames our soul through ideals. In *Faust*, Goethe, who possessed so much intimate wisdom of life, classically expressed the controversy which exists in us between the natural and the higher soul, between the soul which we already possess and the one that still transcends us:

> Two souls, alas! Reside within my breast,
> And each withdraws from, and repels, its brother.
> One with tenacious organs holds in love
> And clinging lust the world in its embrace;
> The other strongly sweeps, this dust above,
> Into the high ancestral spaces.

It opens profound insight into the secrets of existence when we observe how Goethe is led just at this point to have Faust speak of the sphere of higher entities. The struggle for the higher soul touches the sphere of the Angels:

> If there be airy spirits near,
> 'Twixt Heaven and Earth on potent errands fleeing,
> Let them drop down the golden atmosphere,
> And bear me forth to new and varied being!

Faust calls on the Angels for help. It is the soul-element of the Angels, the spirit-self, that he aspires to in his desire for purification. Here, the Angel of the human being permeates himself with man's own higher soul being. We must not form far-fetched, fantastic conceptions of the Angels. We are much closer to their sphere than we normally think.

Doesn't the angel-mystery of the human being confront us graphically in every child? The child does not as yet have a soul of its own. What lives in it as soul, is still the totality. As turbulent as the soul contents of children may often be, what is soul in children is still under the protection of celestial figures and configurations. Within them, the angels are still directly effective. Here, the difference between lower and higher soul is immaterial. One cannot really say of children that two souls dwell in their breast. Truly, children are still under the wings of the angels; by their very nature they have the angelic sphere around them. Only when they grow up and acquire a soul body of their own around age fourteen and finally becomes an adult, the remarkable condition of being sheltered under the wings of the angels has ceased. The tragic separation and controversy begin between the soul we possess and the one that hovers above us, still being borne by our angel. Due to the encapsulation of his being, man is more than ever separated from his higher self and angel. But through the matured ego-power, he should now be in a position to overcome the spell of separation.

What can the adult human being do to open up to the higher soul, the first higher member of his being? Similar to the child, a *praying person* is linked with their angel. When adults practice devotion, the state of eternity and stillness of soul, which is really the essence of prayer, their angel glides down to them. Why? Because their own spirit self, their own true being is close, when they submerges themselves devoutly in prayer. Today, the ability for this has become rare in the world. The tyranny of unrest rules everything. But anyone who now and then takes a few minutes or quarter of an hour of innermost peace and devotion from this tyrant need ask no longer whether angels exist and what they are all about. He can know from experience. The characteristic mark for the fact that the sphere of the angels descends upon the human being is 'peace.' There is no inner peace for man without contact with the sphere of the angels.

Man without the angel can only be a troubled being, a victim of nervousness and all those symptoms of disorders that appear today in almost epidemic fashion as consequences of inner turmoil. It is not merely a personal but a cultural necessity for people today to learn once more the art of inner quiet and prayer before new altars. In this way, they enter into a healing bond between themselves and the angels.

This is the secret of heavenly relationship between the child and praying man, namely that through prayer-filled devotion man becomes a child again on a higher level, for in us is born a part of our higher being that rests in God. Thus, childhood corresponds with 'sonship to God' which is the beginning of all religious life. Where this stage is not first reacquired, one cannot even speak of religion, much less Christianity. This is why the renewal of ritual life is so important, because it is an important school of devotion, contemplation and thus, peace. Formerly, many people could pray because of a childlike frame of mind that had survived through the ages. Today hardly any remnants of this remain. It will therefore be all the more important if modern man, having lost his childlike quality, learns to cultivate the garden of a quite newly-acquired Christian attitude and angelic bond.

One observation will be that if this miracle is reintroduced into human life, the quality of sleep in particular will change. In sleep, our self together with the soul sheath, on which the former works, disengage. We are still far from penetrating our soul sufficiently with our spirit in order to become aware of our self during the night. Still, at night, when we are outside with our soul, we are borne close to the life of the angels. For when the glimmer of a true religious life, the reverberations of genuine prayer are present in us, then, the spirit-selfhood germinates, and our spirit-illumined soul will lovingly be greeted and accepted by the choirs of angels. Here, the true future of humanity arises. And how important will such a healing sanctification of sleep become for an age in which sleep does not even bestow physical reinvigoration to a person attuned only to the earthly-physical dimension!

Wherever images appear in religious terminology such as: 'Spread out your wings ... and take your fledgling in,' or 'I feel sheltered as if in God's bosom,' we are dealing with angelic experiences that emerge from sleep, from having been sheltered at night. In a certain sense, these were the culmination of religious life in past centuries. All too quickly, one spoke of 'God' or 'Jesus' then. But the reality one touched was the spirit-self sphere that is the level of the Angels. The angel of devotion keeps watch there and waits for the human soul.

*

The next sphere is ruled by quite another quality. We draw near it if we not only breathe in as we become quiet within, but when we breathe out again and move from resting to doing. It is then that we work with our *life-forces;* we bring our life-sheath, our formative-forces body into motion. But in what kind of a relationship do we stand today to our life-forces? We say: *'I* live,' but actually we can only say: 'I *live.'* Only rarely is there justification to say: *'I* live,' for in most instances we *are being* lived. The course of the day lives on its own. The alarm clock, hunger at noon and so on take care of that; we humans are rarely the true subjects of our own course of life. Naturally,

when I say, '*I* live,' this need not yet be something very noble.
I can say this based on egotistic self-emphasis. I would have to
think in the Pauline manner: 'I live, but not I, something higher lives in me.' Then I would begin to seek and find a connection to that sphere from which, along with the future forces of
my own higher being, the forces of hierarchical beings come to
my aid. Here, where I look for the spiritualization of my life
body, I sense something of man's second, higher member of
being which is the life element of the Archangels, namely the
life spirit.

One frequently speaks flippantly of 'inner liveliness,' but
what is it? We value it and wish for it but really know inner liveliness only in so far as it shows itself through our own tem-
perament. And if I am a phlegmatic, deliberate person, I may
perhaps envy those people who by their very nature are lively.
But this natural inner liveliness is of no use to us in our spiritual striving. Here we encounter a tragic limitation of human
nature. We can try to enliven and stir up our life forces based on
our ideals and spiritual goals, but in so doing, we really
encounter death. Death is the wages of sin. While we can shape
and develop our soul through our own effort, we cannot do
likewise with our life body. Here, the shadow of original sin
falls on us. We encounter death at the very point where we
would allow life to pour forth out of the spirit.

A short digression may be inserted here. Grasping the reality
of the supersensory aspects of human nature, does not give certainty concerning life after death. Every world view that
includes the supersensory, describes to us that man, having laid
aside his physical sheath at death, loses his life sheath as well a
short time later. What we possess in the way of natural life, we
do not retain for eternity. For one who has perceptions to this
level, the question, 'What really is *life* after death?' becomes
weighty. What is life a few days after physical death, when we
have laid aside our life body? After death, we have at our dis-

posal only the life that we were able to take hold of, make our own and penetrate inwardly with the self; in fact only what we have acquired in the way of transformed life force, spirit-pervaded life force, namely, 'life spirit.' But we cannot struggle to attain life spirit on our own. Here, the mystery of resurrection confronts us. Christ's resurrection after three days is the pivotal miracle of history for the reason that a form of life was thereby inaugurated that no longer originates out of nature. It is a life infused through and through with spirit. How did the resurrection of Christ come about? When we say that Christ vanquished death after three days, we form the conception of an inner struggle that did not begin just at Golgotha, but lasted throughout the whole life of Jesus of Nazareth. A flame-like inner activity finally culminates in the victory of life, the impulse of resurrection. As the fruit of the transformation of natural life, 'eternal life' was here attained and wrested away from the forces of death. Only through Christ's resurrection does 'life' after death exist in actual truth. It is the sphere of the 'life spirit' in which we as Christians can acquire a first share.

With this, we touch a new sphere. This is not the sphere of the Angels but of the Archangels. Here we have to take a step that corresponds to the one by which a child becomes a youth and then an adult. The condition of being a child of God must change to one of being a son of God. Here, we make contact with forces that do not simply result from quiet receptivity and devotion. A fire must penetrate us. We must develop an inner activity that Paul calls *faith.* Faith is not something that one acquires and lives by at the expense of reason. Likewise, it is not just mere feeling that one lets stream out of the heart. It is intervention of a higher spiritual power in our life forces. The resurrection-effect of faith consists of man's bearing in his natural life forces the seed of 'eternal life,' a life that cannot even be taken from him after death. Here, we cannot merely continue to think of the hierarchies in the image of the guardian angel. We have to remember the role angels play in John's Apocalypse, where they are militant spirits. Under certain conditions, filled with mighty activity, they are even the instruments of God's 'wrath.' Here we have to rise to the sphere of the Archangels who are the *geniuses of courage.*

Let us proceed from prayer. In prayer, we can perhaps reach the point of sensing: there is a being, I hear a being, I connect with my angel and the higher spheres he transmits to me. But then I must have the courage to look around for the one who speaks to me, as John does in the Apocalypse, and to address him with inner activity. In so doing, I make the move, in a manner of speaking, from Angel to Archangel. But then I moreover have to gather the courage to know, a courage that is lacking wherever I have become used to the separation of faith and knowledge. I have to call forth the courage of knowing out of faith so that the eye of vision, of knowing, will open. In the name of Christianity it becomes a duty to establish and acquire a world view that encompasses the supersensory as well. Everything now depends on the courage of inner action.

Here, the greatest disorientation holds sway today. People believe that if they do something, that is, if they progress from theory to practice, something has been gained. In reality, our form of doing things in the world has weakened souls in all directions. Outward activity greatly exceeds inward creativity. The drive of unrest is called diligence and hard work. The more busily the wheel of outer activity turns, the more incapable of inner activity we become. So long as things keep rolling we feel energetic, but when we sit at home and have nothing to do and cannot even relax with a newspaper, radio or television, we are miserable. Inner activity that gives all outer activity its significance in the first place is only possible if human beings connect with the sphere of higher life, with the sphere of the Archangels. I can do ever so much but all these activities may be nothing but evading the deeper feeling of inner paralysis. Then at times, mere outward activity can weaken the soul. There are successful people who are mentally quite lazy and cannot even start one thing. None but Christianity can bring about an era where people know once more about the miracle of inner activity, of inner ardour by which death is vanquished and through which human beings attain freedom through the power of the Archangel. Inner *freedom* is given us by the Archangel, even as the Angel gives us *peace*. In this way we gain access to the etheric world, to the sphere of life where Christ reveals himself anew. It is the sphere out of which, through the agency of the Archangel Michael, new Christ-encounters will come into our age.

*

The final thing in the distant future is that the human being will bear a higher, spiritual corporeality. This will be when, three aeons hence, man will embody the third higher member of being, spirit man, in himself. That is the element of the Archai, the Primal Powers, the Spirits of Personality. who stand above the Angels and Archangels. They not merely rule over individual destinies nor the destinies of nations, they reign over a whole epoch. What kind of a mystery is this? I would like to quote words that two contemporaries expressed about Schiller, because these remarks offer at least an indication. Schiller was indeed a torch-bearer; through his soul shimmered the forces of the Archangel and the power of the Time Spirit. The first quote is by Goethe who wrote this to a friend when he was eighty-two years old. Schiller had been dead for twenty-five years. Goethe wrote these words down on the day when Schiller would have been seventy-one years old. But this is unimaginable: Schiller could not become seventy-one years old! It would not have fit his nature. Goethe on the other hand could become this old and older. The eighty-two-year-old writes: 'In Schiller, this Christ-tendency was inborn; he did not touch anything profane without ennobling it.' A shimmer of spirit man, of the spiritualized corporeality, of matter transformed by spirit, this is what was experienced as an effect of Schiller's nature.

Novalis, as a nineteen-year-old, wrote exactly the same thing when Schiller was still alive and only thirty years old: 'Destiny bestowed on him the divine gift of transforming everything he touches into the property and legacy of ethical grace.'

He is referring to the beauty, the charm of moral virtue that illuminates Schiller's environment. Novalis continues and cannot but link his view of Schiller with higher hierarchical beings: 'Schiller, who is more than millions of ordinary men, who could engender in beings devoid of craving whom we call spirits, the wish to become mortals ...' He means: if Angels and Archangels had looked down upon Schiller, it would have aroused in them the will to become human. 'I recognized in him the higher genius who reigns over centuries, and willingly and amiably embraced the command of destiny.' This means that in Schiller's presence the younger Novalis felt as if the Spirit of the Age had become human in Schiller. Particularly in connection with this hint of spirit-man, of transformed matter, the image emerges of the Time Spirit, the hierarchy that stands above the Archangels.

Today, Michael is the spiritual regent of the whole age. He has grown beyond the rank of an Archangel. We touch him when we sense the third mystery. When we touch the Angel, it can help us *to come to ourselves*, for all of us are not yet fully our selves. Only when we make contact with the Angel are we truly in our selves. Only when we connect ourselves with the Archangel *we grow* in truth *beyond our selves*. And this, every human being wants who senses human dignity. But when we touch the sphere of Michael, the time spirit, we learn *to stand within our age*, and that means *to rise above mundane matters*. The

Angel of devotion causes hearts to be peaceful, he bestows *peace*. The Archangel of courage steels the inner will, he gives *freedom*. The Primal Power of Transformation, the Genius of the Age, Michael, creates a new human community with the seeds of spirit-corporeality; he inaugurates true, humanity-encompassing *love*.

Michael, Lord of Progress

Living as we do in a new Michael-age, the Michael-festival is a new festival in so far as we may celebrate it. Its star is just rising and will acquire its full radiance only in the future. The increasingly serious world conditions that attest to the apocalyptic words of the Gospel, namely, that distress will rule among humankind, fear and trembling in the face of what will come to pass over all the earth, will help us to grasp the new content of the Michael festival more clearly year by year.

While the childlike pictures that former centuries produced of the victor over the dragon can still tell us much, they do not show us the Archangel in his present form. They do not allow us to sense the current urgency of his being. The significant features and contours of the new Michael-image ray forth from the solemn words that are spoken during the weeks of Michaelmas-time at the altars of the Christian Community. They are words of adoration, but a drama unfolds in them. The lofty radiant being to whom we let stream our deepest devotion reveals himself at the same time as the bearer of a dramatic tension. In the great steps of humanity's dynamic development we find that once Michael stood before God the Father, today he stands before God the Son. We are to consider a world-historic step that will lead humanity into completely new territory, for the Archangel is a being who does not stand still. And it is not only the fact that he moved in grand style ahead when the time of the Father was replaced by that of the Son. It has happened and happens in our age that Michael's gesture changes: the hand that was stretched out belligerently in threatening manner against the enemy forces is now raised in a beckoning gesture as a sign of poised greatness that counts on the free human being. The angelic Lord of advances to be attained by the inner-most being of man — that is Michael.

This is furthermore the reason for Michael's infinitely dynamic closeness and relationship to Christ. The traditional conception of the deity generally views the divine as remaining in eternal invariability. From this, it is thought that unchange-able religious traditions and forms are to be derived. It is cer-tainly quite possible through such a conception to grasp some-thing of the nature of the Father-God, the Divine Ground of the World. But as yet it does not allow the emergence of an essen-tial feeling for the nature of Christianity. Christ, the Son, is not unchangeable. He is the being who causes all progress in the world, because from the very beginning he has been on his mighty journey and involved in all-encompassing transforma-tion. Even prior to the Event on Golgotha, time and again he left new effects on the ages by journeying towards earth-humanity from sphere to sphere. And after the three years of his life on earth, he did not remain in the condition which — as people presume — he had entered on the fortieth day after Easter. The image of the one who ascended to heaven only indicates that a never-ending further evolution has now begun. The right Christian question therefore is: where is Christ today and how does he work?

The main feature of the never resting, forward-striving advance that is the Christ-being's characteristic nature becomes more distinct and familiar to us the more we succeed in arriv-ing at an image of the present form of the Archangel Michael. Just as did John the Baptist in the earthly world of humans, so Michael opens up the pathways for Christ in the spiritual cos-mos that belongs to humanity. This never-standing-still that is part of the nature of Christ must above all determine the nature of the one who walks before him, moving all obstacles out of the way.

The time in the lofty Michaelic biography when the Archangel 'stood before the Father-God' reflects richly into the Old Testament. The book by the Prophet Daniel still speaks in such a fashion that we realize: until the time of the Babylonian exile, Michael was the genius of the people of Israel (chapters 10, 13 and 21). Through his inspiring guidance, the inner history of the Israelites can be seen as the earthly correspondence to the stages of progression of Christ in the supersensory worlds.

It was actually the Michaelic guidance that turned the folk of the Old Testament into the 'chosen people.' For a number of centuries, the accent and focal point of humanity's evolution rested with the Hebrews. As the vanguard of this evolution that represented all of humanity, the Hebrews had to secure its progress.

In regard to the body, the Israelites had to develop in such a manner that they could eventually offer the possibility of incarnation to Christ who was on his way to the earth. But above all, by acquiring a certain soul force, they had to attain the specific inner progress in human nature through which mankind would one day be capable of taking hold of the working of Christ freely and in full awareness. As the earthly path of Christ had to lead to the Place of the Skull, to Golgotha, the inner evolution of humanity had to lead in the same way to the site of the skull, even if that brought along impoverishment and inner withering. The thinking that is bound to man's head and brain, that makes us poor but likewise free, had to be attained for humanity by the 'chosen people.'

Even though Michael is the Archangel of the sun, when Christ sent him from his pre-earthly sphere of existence ahead as his forerunner, the Archangel had to become the spiritual guide of a people who had a lunar mission, namely, to develop

the moonlike head-reasoning for humanity. As yet, the light of
the spiritual sun, the sunlight of the Christ-entity that was
dawning, could not directly meet and appear to humanity. The
human being was not yet mature enough, but was still too pli-
ant and indistinct. Thus, for a certain duration, the folk had to
become the representative folk of humanity who, with the
moon-forces in their soul, put up the mirror in which the
approaching sunlight reflected indirectly and in subdued form.
What is the moon in the sky? The moon does not shine but
reflects the sunlight like a mirror when the sun is below the
horizon. Through the people who were led by Michael, humanity received Christ's sunlight through the subdued lunar reflection. Human beings learned to acquire universal reason by
head-thinking. Similar to moonlight, brain-bound thought consists of reflected sunlight, mirror-images of universal reason.
This means that we form shadow- and mirror-images of the
divine world of ideas in our brain.

Instead of saying that Michael originally stood in front of the
Father-God, one can likewise say that he had been the countenance of Yahweh before he became the countenance of Christ.
Yahweh is a being that we can picture in the image of the moon,
just as the sun is the mighty image of Christ. As paradoxical as
it may seem, the Archangel of the sun became the countenance
of a moon-deity so that, when the time would be fulfilled, he
could be the direct countenance of the spiritual sun, the Christ-
entity.

*

There is a reason why humanity today is so far from having a
true understanding of Michael's nature. People essentially view
the meaning of history in the sequence of outward events, in the
shift of power-structures, in the successes and failures of human
accomplishments and striving. As yet, they do not pay proper

attention to the fact that a most important aspect of hisstory lies in the evolution of consciousness. The genius and leader of humanity through the various metamorphoses of consciousness is the Archangel Michael. Rudolf Steiner taught us to view him as the 'guardian of cosmic intelligence.' And in this capacity he is the closest servant and trailblazer of Christ.

Early on, Greek thinkers from Heraclitus to the Stoics, knew the Christ-being and — just as the prophets of the Old Testament — had presentiments of his coming. They called him the 'Logos,' just as later the Gospel of John called him. The name 'Logos' does not simply mean 'Word.' It indicates the sphere of origin where the thinking of God and his speech are still one. In a manner of speaking, in the very beginning the garment or spirit-body of the Christ-being consisted of the creative primal thoughts of God, thoughts that we hesitantly could call 'world reason' or 'cosmic intelligence.' The spiritual sun, Christ, in comparison to which the sun in the outer firmament is merely a metaphor, consists of radiant thoughts of God, and Michael is the herald and helper of the Logos. He sees to it that on each level of evolution the right things are always accomplished so that, finally, universal reason itself can directly shine forth from the human spirit. An important intermediate point on this course was the development of the head-bound, intellectual thinking in the Israelite folk-stream that was mightily inspired through Moses, who for that reason was depicted with the two horns on his forehead. The lunar pattern of universal reason began, the Archangel of the sun served the moon. The genius of gold coined silver. He did this because only by passing through the shadowy intelligence of the head could the human being develope a conscious self, an ego, which subsequently can be the free bearer of a higher thinking. The Yahweh-mission was necessary for the preparation of the Christ-mission. And this was why Michael was the countenance of Yahweh before he could turn into the countenance of Christ.

*

The actual history of the Old Testament folk ceased when, following the destruction of the kingdom of the ten tribes of Israel, the Kingdom of Judah, which consisted of the remaining two tribes, was likewise crushed by the Assyrians and the period of the Babylonian exile began. The actual Yahweh-mission was at an end. Michael loosened his ties to that particular folk-stream and rose from the rank of folk-spirit to that of time-spirit. A Michael-epoch commenced. Once again, the solar character of Michael could become directly evident. The whole horizon lit up. Sunrise extinguished the moonlight. Even earlier, among the great Israelite prophets, the view towards the sun had became essential. The Messianic prophecies dominated their proclamation. The first rays of Christ's coming became visible from the distance: daybreak approached.

Michaelic inspiration now reached humanity all around the world. In Greece, the great thinkers from Pythagoras to Plato and Aristotle were contemporaries of the prophets. In India, there was the Gautama Buddha, in Persia, Zarathustra, in China, Lao-tzu and Confucius. The worldwide gathering of great minds was like a Messianic dawn.

When the pivotal event of mankind's history on earth occurred, the Incarnation of Christ, his Death and Resurrection, the Michael-epoch had already ended. The heraldic torches that had blazed forth everywhere burned out. The first step of the re-ascent of humanity's descending evolution occurred in obscurity. We have to imagine a most intimate, delicate connection between the Archangel Michael and the events as reported by the Gospel. Nothing directly is said of it, but when lightning flashes through the quiet scenes of Galilee, we behold the countenance of Michael as through a cloud, participating in what was happening on the earth.

The Archangel stood before the Father-God, now he stands

before God, the Son. He is the countenance of Christ and is preparing to become the countenance for human beings. The goal of these efforts will be attained when, not shadowed and darkened by head-thinking, the sunlight of divine thoughts finds direct entry into human souls. Following the event on Golgotha, the Michaelic Christ-future flashes up here and there: before Damascus for Paul, on Patmos for John.

But the history of Christianity weaves a heavy veil in front of the light that has rayed forth all along. Christ's sun-nature is hidden to Christians. They only see the human being, Jesus. The insight that the relationship to Christ could have an effect on human consciousness, on human thinking, is remote to them. They are becoming increasingly accustomed sharply to detach faith from knowledge. The Michaelic longing for a direct Christ-vision sheds light merely into solitary seekers of God.

Once again, to an increasing degree, the Archangel influences the dynamics of historical development in the service of the Christ-future. During the ages of the folk migrations, certain tribes felt themselves to be under his guidance and looked up to him reverently. As he had done in the times of the Old Covenant, so now Michael made ready to assume a folk-task once more. The ethnic groups who felt themselves to be under his leadership evolved into one people. But it would not be correct to say simply that Michael had become the folk-spirit of the Germans. He hovered over the folk that developed in central Europe but did not pervade the blood-configuration of these people to the same degree as he had done in regard to the folk of the Old Covenant. Thus, in German cultural history, Michael's folk-soul-effects actually lit up only in individuals such as in Fichte, Hegel, Schelling or in Goethe, people in whom thought tried to break loose from the level of mere reflections and shadow-images. This time, the folk-soul-effect of Michael does not aim towards preparing the physical birth of Christ. In a segment of humanity, a spiritual atmosphere is supposed to be created through which originates an openness for the *new* Coming of Christ. Through the Michaelic guidance, the whole of the German cultural history has in fact had the purpose of creating the foundation for the new Christ-revelation that is customarily termed Christ's 'Second Coming.'

It does not signify a waning of the Michael-influences in the second half of the nineteenth century that the lights of the Goethean period went out so utterly and had to yield to an increasing darkening through the rule of mere head-reason. The counter-effects grew, but quietly the Michaelic power grew too.

Finally, on the stage of outer history, there occurred a tragedy similar to the one when the Jews were caught up in the Babylonian exile. In the 1870s, contrary to external appearances, German folk history had by now come to an end. Michael rose once again from his folk-spirit-role to a time-spirit-task. To the German spirit, the task was posed to develop beyond the dimension of folk-egoism and rise to selfless, all-encompassing humanitarian service.

*

In the new Michael-age that began in 1879, we have experienced the gigantic expansion of the counter-forces. Day after day, we have to endure their messages of victory and triumph that basically just increase the inner dismay and torment of human souls, the shivers of fear of what is yet to come.

But we have likewise become witnesses to the beginnings of new Michaelic inspiration. The first great gift by Michael for our age was Rudolf Steiner's lifework. If humanity has the courage to make these gifts their own, they will be armed with sunlike instead of moonlike thoughts. In the midst of the growing, tempestuous darkness, Christ and Michael remain close to humankind, bearing the sun that shines at midnight towards human beings. Where people make the transition from mere head-thinking — without losing the stern discipline of thought that the age of science has brought about — to the creative, Michaelic thoughts conceived jointly by head and heart, there, the seed for beholding the supersensory and with it the Damascus-awakening of the human soul becomes evident.

In the spirit-sphere, Michael's battle with the dragon has been concluded victoriously. On earth, man still has to complete it in alliance with Michael, the countenance of Christ. He does not accomplish this through strenuously battling against the achievements of darkness; he does so through the positive spiritual sovereignty that is inherent in each and every true Christlike insight, in every Christ-pervaded thought.

Michael's gesture is no longer that of battle. He raises his hand beckoning. Free human beings are supposed to heed this gesture. Through all the terrors and through all the dying we can encounter and serve the Easterly sun of the Resurrected One.

Christ and Michael

The arrival of autumn always signifies a test. When, at the end of September, the sun enters the constellation of Libra, humans are in fact weighed on a stern scale: will their inner strength suffice if the support of nature is withdrawn and they are thrown back on themselves?

Today, there is a lesser and a greater autumn: the one that rhythmically recurs in the year's course, and the other of the present epoch that humanity has entered. The greater autumn increasingly exercises its dominion since a summer-period of humanity has irrecoverably come to a close. It even interferes in the year's course by causing the annual autumn to predominate. Rain showers come earlier and there are almost no proper, untroubled summers any more.

Protective veils surrounded us through the warmth-permeated beauty of summer's nature. They are roughly torn away when out of sombre backgrounds, an icy breeze touches us, turbulent downpours thunder around us. If we have the strength firmly to take our stand inwardly, then another form emerges out of the dusky-dark depths at first as a gentle light but then shining more and more brightly: the Archangel Michael. The golden radiance issues from his armour and the scales he holds up in his hand. His lips are sealed, his earnest, caring eye rests upon us humans. His silent apprehension speaks:

'I am here for you, my whole desire is to help you. But if you remain the way you are, I am not allowed to help you. For you would remain even more what you are now. And what you are does not suffice for the world's future. First you have to change, then you can be certain of my support.'

We feel: this form is not simply something outside ourselves. It concerns each one of us in our innermost being. It stands before us like a stern mirror of God and causes us to realize how far we fall short, how weak we are inwardly and how, thereby, we succumb over and over again to the allure of merely outer things.

Not until we honestly sense the earnestness in thus being tested does the Archangel begin his instruction.

*

In the ancient legends the one belonging to the day of Michael started with the listing of the nine angelic hierarchies. September 29 was called, 'St Michael and all Angels.' The view of the hierarchies, from Angels and Archangels all the way to Cherubim and Seraphim is revealed to our soul. Michael stands before us as the representative and herald of the angelic realms and shows them all to us. Hence the first thing that he teaches us silently is this: 'Do not always direct your sight to the kingdoms of nature, widen it to the realms of the spirit. Seek beyond stone, plant, animal and man for the true majesty of existence, all the way to the Seraphim.'

Then it all begins to move. We see 'how heaven's forces rise and fall and hand each other golden vessel.' We feel as did Jacob when once the Archangel opened his dream-eyes so that he saw the ladder to heaven: '... there was a ladder set up on the earth, and the top of it reached to heaven; and behold, the angels of God were ascending and descending on it! And behold, the Lord stood above it' (Gen.28:12f).

What kind of an ascending and descending is this? What

kind of conversation is this between heaven and earth that is not conducted in words but in living being?

Caught up in the prevailing world views, many people can make nothing of it when Angels, Archangels and others are mentioned. They are concerned that the perception of hierarchical beings could diminish the grand concept of the One God. They do not wish to stand before a multitude but only before the exalted Oneness.

The mighty divine universe, however, appears to us in an unimaginable living manifoldness when, following Michael's gesture, we turn our gaze to the ascending and descending heavenly forces who, after all, do not stop at the level of the Angels, but pass on their golden vessels to man, animal, plant and stone. They are all limbs on the body of a deity, and so are we along with all of earth's creatures. When, looking back on our life, we say: we have sensed the hand of God in our destiny, this is not merely a pictorial expression. The Angels, assigned as they are as protective and guiding geniuses to individual human beings, are truly the hands of God. We can call the Archangels arms, the Thrones the feet of God. And Christ is the heart of God. We sense that the mighty oneness and the rising and falling movement within the multiplicity is like the pulsating, living blood circulation in the one mighty being.

This divine blood circulation should likewise pass through us humans. But through the 'Fall,' the tragic schism appeared in Creation: man has pulled earth's creatures along into separation from God. We begin to comprehend Michael's instruction that would like to lead us from mere observation of separated outer nature to true self-knowledge and from there to a new perceptive connection to the world of the spirit. He would like to turn his instruction into an awakening.

*

In the immense organism that encompasses heaven and earth, Michael too has the function of a certain organ. Because of this, he even stands above the hierarchies who are higher in rank than he. He can thus be Herald and Lord of all Angels. He is the 'Countenance of Christ.' What is meant by that?

Michael is a living example of a fundamental life-principle to all beings above and below, a principle that can link all the spheres, from the depths up to the greatest heights, the principle of *openness to above*. The full truth of each evolutionary level is completely revealed only in the fact that it is open to the next higher level. Angels must be open to the Archangels, the Archangels to the Archai, and so on. Each level must be so unselfish that it becomes an organ for the higher order. None may wish to be there only for itself. In superhuman, exalted fashion, Michael makes the sentence come true which, in analogy with Paul, we put into the words, 'Not I, but Christ in me.' He says: Christ in me; thus does Christ dwell in him. Out of Michael's eyes, Christ looks upon us, on Michael's brow shine the thoughts of Christ. And were he to open his earnestly silent lips, then Christ would speak through him. This is what the saying, 'Michael is the countenance of Christ' refers to.

We modern humans need to understand the secret of 'interweaving,' of true integration. A conception of God, with Angels and higher entities, standing side by side or even confronting each other, is quite inadequate now. Then we would wait for the moment when this higher being, perhaps God himself, comes towards us and does something for us. The basic principle of Creation is a mighty and sacred interweaving. 'What kind of God would it be who would only press from without ...?' We can speak with Paul: 'Not I, but Christ in me!' And when this word is fulfilled, then, through Christ, the Father likewise begins to live in us. The rule of the indwelling is the very heart-principle of the Christian world view.

Someone who only wishes to be himself, be it in egotistical behaviour or in superficial thinking, or rather lack of thinking about himself, is *not* truly himself. If we are only that which we are, then we are not yet truly human, we are not yet even truly ourselves. Man only begins to be truly man when he is open to a higher being. And whether we then speak of the angel of man or of his true higher self — it is initially merely a tentative searching for the truth but a searching for one of the most important truths of our existence. Alertness is, however, required here. True it is that one, in whose countenance the radiance of the genius does not shine, is merely a fragment or even a caricature of a human. But if the entity to whom we open up is in turn not open itself to what is above it, we merely arrive at a glittering semblance of higher spirit. We are then not truly open in a selfless manner. Our vanity and ambition attract a Luciferic spirituality into our soul, not one that serves Christ.

As yet, we do not possess within ourselves what is intended for us as our true being. That being still hovers above us. This is why we have to unite with the angelic choirs that ascend and descend on the ladder of heaven, because they still bear and harbour our true being.

*

The principle of indwelling passes through all the levels of existence wherever none but selfless openness prevails to what is above.

The being whom we call by the name 'Christ' has been the classic primal image and archetype of this openness since time immemorial. As anthroposophy describes it, in those times Christ and Lucifer were still brothers who belonged to the same hierarchical level. Eventually, a moment arrived in the great

evolutionary course of the universe, when a being of this hierarchical rank had to be open to receive the Logos, the Word of
the Worlds, through whose resounding our Creation had its
beginning. Christ was open to what was above, and the Logos,
the Son-principle, entered him. Lucifer wished to be himself
and to utilize the power of the Logos for his own purposes.
Because of his selfish action, he lost his rank and hold and fell
away. In many folk sagas, a reminiscence still survives of the fall
of Lucifer. It occurred at the very moment, when Christ was elevated to be the bearer of the Logos and thus to be the organ for
the Creation of our world.

*

Christians in earlier times always were in the habit of saying,
Dominus vobiscum, 'The Lord be with you,' in their services.
Today, adhering to the Pauline Christian principle of indwelling, we say, 'Christ in you.' The ancient formulation is not
wrong. But it really applies to a childhood-stage of humanity.
One can say to a child, 'May your angel be with you.' The
guardian angel protects the child from dangers, hovering above
the child at night and accompanying him during the day. But
when the human being grows up, the relationship to his angel
changes. The angel dismisses us from the earlier guardianship
because we are to become free beings. The angel no longer helps
us from outside without our having a hand in it. A grown person can remain in contact with their angel only if, in true openness that is directed upwards, they admit the angel into heart
and mind. And above all, once we have become adults, we cannot assume that Christ would work miracles on us from outside. Only if we learn to say, 'Christ in me,' can we count on his
blessings. The gifts of Christ are meant to be received inwardly,
not just in a passively receptive manner but through the active
receptivity that we call 'faith.'

We grow into a great, fulfilled, Christian future if the words, spoken at the altar, 'Christ in you' and 'Christ in us' are increasingly accompanied by activity of soul and finally become the aim and content of personal devotional efforts. Regular immersion into the sphere of devotion of ritual life of the congregation, and faithfully practised prayer in the life of the individual support the 'openness to above.' Thus, through the genuinely kindled fire of faith, love and hope, there will truly take place what the words at the altar ask for in prayer, namely, Christ's entry into the human soul.

What will quite certainly happen to start with, if we practice this, is that our angel who bears our higher self, moves into us. And through him, a living communication reaches us, an echo of grace, a reflection of grace out of the Christ-sphere. The more we then attain the active permeable condition that allows our higher self to enter into our earthly self, the more the angel will become for us, in a manner of speaking, the 'countenance of Christ.' And inasmuch as the indwelling of Christ lights up in the angel, it takes place in us as well.

This is the first stage, the stage of being 'children of God,' for which we have to struggle ever and again in a genuine, child-like attitude of piety. The step from child to sonship is taken when not only the Angel but also the Archangel, who in the real sense is the 'countenance of Christ,' begins to fulfil and penetrate us. We experience the proximity and power of the Archangel Michael, and due to this the new form of Christ's nearness and power. A little of this always becomes evident if we feel urged upon not to retain the higher power awakening in us for ourselves, but actively to prove it in the service of the 'growing kingdom of God.'

What initially touched us in feeling, made us quiet and filled our inner tranquillity, now wishes to take hold of our will. Schiller coined the words: 'Receive the deity into your will and it will step down from its universal throne.' Does this not sound to the ears of most Christians like irreverent boldness and presumptuous audacity by man against God? In reality it shows that Schiller knew something of the Pauline Christian principle of indwelling, even though in formulating the verse itself he may not have thought of making a Christian or religious statement. In fact, he points to the secret of indwelling in the *Michaelic* sense here. Christ as the Logos, the Son, who includes man in the sonship, is the Creator of the world. If we learn to speak and act 'in Christ's name,' 'in the Lord's name,' we can turn into bearers of a higher creator-faculty by the Grace of God.

*

Now, it is not just that the Michaelic inclination simply enters into the Christian attitude through the step from feeling to will and deed. The Archangel Michael is not so much concerned with deeds of the outer kind but rather *deeds of consciousness.* He is the Lord of unfolding, an unfolding that leads humans out of their blindness of the spiritual world to a new spirit-perception. Owing to the Fall, the Twilight of the Gods had descended upon humanity's ancient vision of God, but at the same time this allowed man to acquire freedom. The purely intellectual head-consciousness is the midnight-condition in humanity's great evolution of consciousness. With all his strength, Michael is trying today to lead the human soul to a new sunrise.

This is why his forward-urging interest is not directed to the will in general. His concern is *the will in thinking,* the will which frees our life of thought and cognition from the mere head-element. This will permeates the life of thought and cognition with the warmth of the heart's lifeblood and releases it with all the power at our disposal from the bonds that tie it to the sense world, freeing it for the supersensory.

The more we become familiar with Michael's being, the more directly will it speak to us as the *'countenance-being,'* and particularly in the time since Christ's Death and Resurrection, as the *countenance of Christ.* In the human being, the countenance is the place of wakefulness and consciousness: through the wakeful eye, the brightest of our sense organs; through the clear brow through which our thoughts can shine; through the mouth with which we can express in distinct words what we think, feel and will. If the force of Michael's influence reaches us, it must become evident in the end in a transforming way in our perception, thinking and in our speech. And since Michael is the 'Countenance of Christ,' he directs Christ's indwelling in us towards our consciousness. He himself lets Christ live in him in such way, that in his perceiving, thinking and speaking Christ himself sees, thinks and speaks. Thus, in the souls of those who draw near to Christ in the Michaelic sense, he frees the way so that, through our human eye too, Christ can see, through our forehead Christ can think, and through our mouth Christ can speak. The Christianization of the heart is always the beginning of being Christian. But Michael's aim is that the activity of our head which bears our countenance is likewise Christianized.

The dividing line between faith and knowledge had to be drawn once in the course of human history, because, for a while, during the midnight of the evolution of consciousness, heart and head had to go their different ways. But the period during which the coldness of head-thinking contradicted the warmth of the pious heart must come to an end today. Michael struggles for the Christianization of thinking and perception, something that is based on the heart's participation in the functions of the head. A Christianity of consciousness must be won from the autumn of humanity in which faith-filled perception and perceptive faith once again link humans fully with the angelic hierarchies, whose Lord and herald is Michael.

If we say, 'Christ in us' in the right way, then Christ begins to live in our hearts.

If Michael says, 'Christ in me,' his countenance is illumined as the countenance of Christ.

If we say with Michael, 'Christ in us,' then Christ begins to be active in our heart *and* in our head.

The Michael-Thought:
Festival of What is Developing

The Michaelic element that we have to learn to find and feel in a completely new way never lies in what has developed and is finished. It always lies in what is developing, in an ideal perfection for which we must struggle.

It is not as simple as some may imagine to form a picture of Michael, the Archangel. None of the depictions of earlier centuries apply any more. We may no longer be tied down to these images. Instead we must learn to find the Archangel where he stands *today*, having left behind all his former stages of activity. The Michaelic element today may rather be experienced like a wind that blows through the world; like a widespread mood that wishes to take hold of human hearts; perhaps even like a storm, though we must not be afraid of it. To create a finished human-like picture of him, all too easily diverts from the elementary, global, all-pervasive nature of Michael's effects.

How does Michael speak today? He does not speak in words. His language is one of closed lips; it is a language of emanation, of atmosphere, of an attitude of will. In particular, we must understand today that even though he is the Archangel of the sun, he does not speak through the seasons of spring and summer, but through autumn. For he does not speak through the ascending life of nature, he does not speak out of what can be given from outside to the human being. He speaks solemnly; he speaks in a manner that shows he always trusts humans to do something great. He does not want them to be mere receivers who simply wish always to accept something. Those, he generously overlooks. He seeks those who themselves try to bring about what they desire in the world and for the world.

Now, we not only find ourselves in the annual autumn which is introduced year after year through the Michael-time. We confront the great autumn that gives our epoch its character since we have entered upon a Michael age. Often, it even seems as if the great autumn, the autumnal element in all mankind, causes the little annual autumn to come earlier. More and more frequently, it begins when it really should still be summer. Thus, this aspect of autumn that does not enrich us but demands of us inner activity and steadfastness, may well move still more to the foreground. Some years no longer even have a real summer and when we are still looking forward to summer, autumn prematurely sends out its messengers. In coming years, even the so-called beautiful fall-days may fail to appear more often. The world assumes an increasingly stern quality and as sons and daughters of a Michaelic age we have to find a more courageous lifestyle.

Michael neither wishes to give nor spare us anything. He does nothing to console us over the difficulties of life. But it is not as if he had no compassion and wanted to torment us. When hardship befalls people and they encounter great difficulty, he speaks: 'You must grow strong through this. Those who do not grow by it but break under the strain and are too weak to persevere in the trial of the great autumn will perhaps have their turn in a future life, but now I cannot use them.' We can see that when dangers threatened, when for instance, in the Second World War under the continual threat of air raids, and even in the years immediately after the war, human souls were much more open and alive than today. When times of prosperity return, it is as if Michael speaks: 'When you are doing well, I cannot do anything with you!' Everything that comes easily from outside, like summer's bounty and prosperity, is all too easily a hindrance for Michael's intentions unless we make proper use of it. The emphasis of human existence has to be on inner matters. In summer, we travel around in the world as never before. The idea is that one relaxes and recovers in this way. But in the future, we shall find that even the most spectacular scenery can no longer give us the hoped-for restoration of energy. Only through *inner* relaxation, through inner mobility and work will the spent life-forces be refreshed and renewed. In this way, a shifting of summer's landscape to the soul's interior occurs, even if storms rage and endless rain pours down. The inner landscape of summer that arises through the warmth of faithful inner exercise will bestow restoration on the human being.

Michael's glance is always directed towards the future. The past may have brought ever so many great things, nature may still preserve much beauty from its paradisal legacy, but the eye of the Michaelic spirit does not rest on this. He knows that this is coming to an end. But he likewise is aware of the kind of future, in the service of which human beings have to undergo their impoverishment and trials.

Essentially it is not even Michael's intention merely to look back upon what once took place as a historic event on Golgotha. He does not view the Mystery of Golgotha by looking back in history, but views it as something that is of the present and the future. This is why he leads us to a new, higher sensing and understanding of the living deed of death on Golgotha which, in its after-effects, bestows life and light. The event on Golgotha is for Michael first and foremost a key to all the portals of the future. He wants us to recognize that every rightly accomplished death, moves humanity forward; every inner suffering bears fruit. Thus, life constantly blossoms forth from death. The silently expressed word of Michael is that Golgotha is not a content of the past but is a principle of life, is a key to the future, is an inner orientation for humanity's attitude. It is the content of his quiet yet clear call to our age.

*

How does Michael speak to us today in the Bible? There too, he does not speak directly in human words. When we learn to read the Bible not just as edifying single passages, but dramatically as a whole, as drama at the level of our heart, we are led to the speech of Michael. Even the Old Testament guides us in classic manner to find our way to Michaelic speech.

The Old Testament has first the historic books; these are followed by the poetic books including the Psalms, and finally there are the prophetic scriptures. Whether we have the naïve conception that all this emerged from a single source of revelation, or (as uninspired scholars have begun to claim in the past two hundred years) we believe that the books of the Old Testament were recorded at very different times, and thus quickly losing the word of God in the Bible and being merely left with human words, we should really allow the whole structure of the Old Testament to work on us. From the first two groups, the historical books that look into the past and the poetic texts that form the transition to the third group, we move on to the prophetic books that look into the future.

There, even in the history of the Old Covenant, we come across a significant turning-point. The era of the prophets falls in the period when the nation of Israel had become homeless. The kingdom of Israel with its ten tribes and then the kingdom of Judah with the two remaining tribes were destroyed. Thus, the prophetic books of the Old Testament are part of the Michael-age which began when the folk history was at an end.

Earlier, Michael had been the Archangel of the Hebrews. Now, he rose to the rank of Archangel of the age. National history could well break apart. The alien conquerors were allowed to crush the Israelite nation and lead the remaining people into the Babylonian exile. In this new situation, the prophets spoke and through them, Michael. No longer was the view directed to the past as in the books of Moses. Now, the orientation is towards the future, and for this reason the prophetic scriptures all have the dual sound of calamity as well as salvation. The tempests have already begun to rage. The catastrophes of misfortune have by now closed in, and the books of the prophets, particularly that of Jeremiah, but the others as well, are filled with the proclamation: times will become more and more difficult; they will bring with them increasingly dramatic trials, but all this is nothing but the shadow of the One who is coming. In the midst of the turbulence, the prophets were able to turn their gaze towards the Messianic future of humanity.

For more than half a century, we today have again embarked on a Michaelic age. And as the great power blocks came about in the former age, for instance, the Assyrian kingdom and then the Babylonian kingdom, in whose name Nebuchadnezzar shattered Judah and led the rest of the Israelite people into exile, today [1960], too, we have the super-powers divided into East and West, while Europe is politically declining. Politically it no longer can be turned into a power-factor if it does not take hold of its spiritual task. When a Michael-age begins, national ties are always out of date. The national element that we do not acquire but simply possess due to common heritage moves into the background. The national element must become the element of *humanity*. This was true then and today it is true again. National ambitions and power struggles can no longer be beneficial, for they are nothing but a return to relationships of the past. In a Michael-age, the gifts of the past are out of date and no longer relevant. In their place, the gentle blowing of the Michaelic wind, the roaring of the Michaelic storm can pass through humanity and the world. A new spirit-element can be sensed. Initially, indistinctly, becoming ever clearer, an atmosphere pervades that does not offer comfort but addresses our innermost kernel of being.

How is it in the New Testament? Do we not have something in today's Michael-age that corresponds to the reason why the prophets appeared during the breakdown of world conditions in the seventh and sixth pre-Christian century? We can fathom the miracles of Providence that are found as if crystallized in the structure of the New Testament. There too, we have the historical books, the Gospels and the Acts of the Apostles that look back to the events of the three years of Christ's life on earth and the initial Christian developments that followed. Then come the Letters of Paul and in conclusion the Apocalypse. Also with the New Testament we can easily have the feeling that it all flowed out of a single source of revelation, especially since the Fourth Gospel and the Apocalypse go back to the same person, John. Yet, at that time, and particularly because of Paul's Damascus-experience, provisions were made for a future when it will once more become necessary that humanity possesses prophetic texts so as to direct their gaze towards the future. Although it seems at first paradoxical, while the Pauline letters have been in existence for two thousand years, they were really written for *today*. The Revelation to John at the end of the New Testament was recorded as early as the latter part of the first century but was written providentially for *our* time. John's Revelation is the holy scripture for our present Michael-age.

What does it seek to convey? It does not try to refer to one or more isolated events that one puzzles about. Instead, it tries to communicate an overall view of the future. Certainly, we read the Gospels with gratitude and reverence for what occurred during the sacred Three Years. The name Jesus, the name of the human being in whom Christ incarnated, tells us infinitely much; we shall never exhaust what it tells us. But when we mention the Christ-name, we ultimately do not refer to something that belongs in the past. We refer to the Being that today and in the future will increasingly come to life in humanity. We do not only mean he who was, but he who is to come and even today is coming. We look upon his Messianic future even as the people of the Old Testament anticipated the coming of the Messiah during the Babylonian exile. This is really the language of Michael. In the midst of all the trials and tribulations which are meant to waken and strengthen humanity inwardly, the sun of a new Christ-nearness is arising. It is a Messianic future that we are approaching, one that has even now begun.

Yes, let us read the Bible and in reading let us hear — if not in the single words but in the great dramatic structure of the New Testament — the language of Michael, the language of the apocalyptic consciousness! Even though the structure of both the Old and New Testament confronts us only in broad outlines, we stand at the threshold of a new nature. It is a new world of summer and spring in the midst of the cold showers and ominous events of the present that is nevertheless a Michaelic age. And we can say: indeed, the outward summer will no longer yield much; in the course of years it will decrease. The outer sun will help humans less and less, for it has entered upon its declining phase. But there will be more and more of the inner summer, of the emanations of the inner sun. And Michael is the Archangel of the sun in the sense of the inner, spiritual sun. Undaunted, he allows the outer sun to decline, he allows much to become duskier and cold; but it is his concern that the spiritual sun will rise in humanity along with the Second Coming of Christ. And even in winter around the altar flowers will bloom, flowers of the soul, flowers of faith. And human beings will become whole and well if they open to this summer's radiance.

Thus, let us approach with great joyous expectation all that the future holds. Without a doubt, the future may bring many shocking events. But if we listen to Michael's language, the language of the Apocalypse, the future will bring us a new Christ-nearness as well, if only we dare venture out upon the stormy sea of evolution in the Michaelic age.